Mastering Frustration

Dealing with Stress, Anger and Toxic Relationship

Elisha O. Ogbonna

Mastery Frustration: Dealing with Stress, Anger and Toxic Relationship

by Elisha O. Ogbonna

This book was written to provide educational and self-help purposes.

First Published: July, 2020
Revised Edition: May, 2024

Copyright © May 2024 by Elisha O. Ogbonna

All rights reserved. No part of this book may be reproduced, transmitted, or distributed in any form by any means, including, butnot limited to, recording, photocopying, or taking screenshots of parts of the book without prior written permission from the author or the publisher.

ISBN:
978-1-7772771-6-1 (Hardcover)
978-1-7772771-4-7 (Paperback)
978-1-7772771-5-4 (eBook)
978-1-7772771-7-8 (Audio)

Prinoelio Press
For Elisha Ogbonna
https://www.elishaogbonna.com

Dedication

Amanda and Rebecca,
and
to those facing difficult times, striving to emerge strong and fulfilled.

MASTERING FRUSTRATION

Table of Contents

Dedication	3
Introduction:	9

CHAPTER 1
Unveiling the Hidden Foe — 15

CHAPTER 2
The Nature of Human Emotional Energy — 23

CHAPTER 3
The Spectrum of Our Emotional Energy — 33

CHAPTER 4 — 49
Types of Frustration and Stressors — 49

CHAPTER 5 — 63
The Telltale Signs of Frustration — 63

CHAPTER 6 — 77
The Price of Frustration — 77

CHAPTER 7 — 83

Battling with Inner Demons — 83

CHAPTER 8 — 89

Releasing Inner Frustration — 89

CHAPTER 9 — 93

Navigating Workplace Difficulties — 93

CHAPTER 10 — 107

Navigating Frustration in Education — 107

CHAPTER 11 — 115

Navigating Frustration in Relationships — 115

CHAPTER 12 — 143

Dealing with Angry Children — 143

CHAPTER 13

Handling Your Angry Teenager — 151

CHAPTER 14

Navigating the Financial Challenges — 159

CHAPTER 15 — 189

Frustration Management Techniques					189

## CHAPTER 16								199
The Power of Effective Communication				199

CHAPTER 17
Your Frustration Detector					205

CHAPTER 18
Self-Examination – Your Survey					211

CHAPTER 19
Further Self-Help on Frustration Management			215

Epilogue:							219

MASTERING FRUSTRATION

Introduction:

Frustration begins as a quiet whisper and grows deep roots when ignored for a long time. Imagine a scenario where you or someone you know is stuck trying to open a stubborn bottle cap, and it cannot yield your persistent effort to flick it open. Consider how frustrated you would become. Now, picture the impatience as your fingers drum relentlessly against the steering wheel in congested or crawling traffic. Have you ever tried assembling pieces of furniture that came with a manual with unclear instructions or assembling a puzzle over some instruction sheet that is not detailed? Those are all examples of frustration at work.

I did a quality inspector job from 2012 to 2017, during which I was on duty for a visual inspection. I also performed mechanical and functional part verification for computer and automotive parts. After inspecting a product and confirming it meets all quality requirements and standards, I would mark it with a green "verified" tag. If it didn't pass, it would receive a red tag for scrap or a yellow tag for engineering rework.

MASTERING FRUSTRATION

One day, I was preparing to conduct the everyday work of the day alongside a co-worker. My work location for quality inspection was roughly 40 feet from the robotic production cells. This closest robotic cell is the final part before inspection in the production process of this manufacturing plant. On this day, I didn't know that there would be an out-of-the-blue drama that I would later use to show how much effect frustration can have on an individual's life.

Within hours of the work, we heard a loud sound, and within a few minutes, there were more successive sounds of someone banging on something. We were startled and wondered what it was as we turned our heads in the direction of the sound. Surprisingly, a single operator stood in defiance just outside one robot cell. This robot, designed to handle processed parts with finesse and get the part to the next in line, had begun dropping every piece of mass to the floor. The angry employee tried to reboot the unruly robot, a classic "turn it off and back on again" solution.

Red with anger, the man turned to the metal fence where a robot was housed and began using his fist to bang against the door. He was angry and frustrated that a particular robot was not following program instructions and his overwritten commands. Instead of compliance, it would pick an auto part from the robot before it and drop it on the floor instead of handing it to the next robot for processing. Learning that several resets and reprogramming were to no avail, the employee's rage became unbearable as the robot's dysfunction and product wastefulness refused resets and program updates.

As a result of this frustration, in his enraging experience, this worker lost his coolness and rationality in seeking assistance from the supervisor. The more he was caught trying to fix it, the more wasteful the situation became. And he didn't consider asking a coworker either. Every time the robot dropped a part, he would strike the metal cell with his fist out of frustration.

When we intervened and talked to the worker, he realized he had an option. Eventually, however, this worker would find out that he would have more downtime and not meet his day's target. Also, the pain and sores on his fist would take days to heal because he had used his fist to strike the robot's metal cell. This is frustration at its best.

Frustration is a natural and universal response to the obstacles we meet. It affects almost every aspect of our lives, both the outer and inner worlds. Frustration wields a powerful influence and can distort our lives in many ways, from external turmoil to burning anger within, a troublesome relationship with anyone else, and what unfolds in our professional lives. Long-term dissatisfaction in a relationship can create tension and misinterpretations, leading to disconnects between people. Expectations, if not met, could lead to frustration in different situations, such as conflicts and communication breakdowns. In addition to the immediate relationships between you and other people, the negative impact of frustration may spill over to different dimensions of your life, which is also badly needed for healthy living.

A cycle of unresolvable frustration in relationships can trigger adverse effects on mental health. For instance, ongoing conflicts may cause chronic stress, which could eventually lead to a mental health illness. Relationship strain can also take an emotional toll, even if unrelated to other elements of our lives; this emotional turmoil then affects self-esteem and satisfaction with life.

Frustration is like a chaotic and overwhelming storm. Frustration can run deep as a negative emotion; it can break up relationships faster than almost any other feeling, smother dreams quicker than anything else, and lead the way to a wasteful and destructive life. This can lead to a range of serious issues, including family violence, suicide, divorce, job loss, and more. Frustration affects every area of our lives — the workplace, classroom, at home, and with personal endeavors. Some people transform their frustration into a quest for personal evolution, pushing

MASTERING FRUSTRATION

themselves to take risks and grow. In contrast, others embark on an endless wild goose chase that only inflames things and hinders their chances of alleviating difficulties.

Knowing that those feelings of frustration could compound into debilitating consequences demonstrates why it is paramount to recognize your emotional condition as soon as possible to deal with them healthily and live a happy, fulfilled life. Unaddressed frustration can have widespread consequences, affecting not only relationships with loved ones but also one's mental health.

This book will explore the three types of frustration that lead to these emotional experiences and provide us with the characteristics of each. It will show us clear red flags indicating a need for it so that it may avoid catastrophic repercussions and wrap things up on how you manage those demanding situations.

The goal is to provide you with invaluable tools and insights to be aware, nip frustration in the bud, and defeat it. This material will help you understand and manage difficult situations, whether from internal struggles, relationship tension or crisis, family emergencies, or professional tribulations. Remember that emotional well-being, personal growth, and goal achievement revolve around how well you can handle frustration.

MASTERING FRUSTRATION

Chapter 1

Unveiling the Hidden Foe

Frustration is a complex emotional experience that results from challenging encounters. Frustration sets in when people encounter obstacles that impede their speed and truncate their ability to reach their desired goals or meet essential needs. It is characterized by dissatisfaction, disappointment, and distress resulting from the inability to overcome hindrances or attain expected outcomes. The most problematic thing is that frustration can tangibly spill over into all facets of life, from your relationships to work, academic pursuits to personal ambition, or even the quest for things you want.

When we're frustrated, it is A Big Deal. It impacts how our Body and Mind process and respond to things happening to us. Emotions like anger, rage, and anxiety are usually complementary negative feelings associated with frustration. They may escalate into bitterness and hurt. These emotions are natural responses to perceived life's roadblocks or challenges; however, they can slow progress, impair rational reasoning, and ultimately lead one to make the wrong decision.

When frustration triggers heightened emotions, it affects the body by tensing muscles, increasing stress hormone levels, and raising the heart rate. Our bodies respond this way as part of an adaptive mechanism to prepare us for action if we sense danger or difficulty. The feelings of incapacitation, lack of hope, and disappointment are significant causes of personal frustration. Other experiences, like difficulties in winning or finishing a task, can be heartbreaking. Everyone needs support; lack of support, unfruitful engagement, and prolonged disagreements can set off frustration. External factors such as inclement weather, traffic jams in the streets, or machinery breakdowns can negatively affect our emotions and implode patience.

Anger is a complex emotion that evolves and changes, often resulting from frustration. It is not always a criminal impulse but simply an instinct response to perceived threats or injustices that anyone experiences. When situations that do not meet our expectations or are against our planned goal arise, we can become angry. This emotional response might range from moderate annoyance to red-hot, searing anger. How people act when they are angry and the results of their actions can provide us with several examples of the consequences that uncontrolled anger carries. The repercussions of anger can be irrecoverable, especially when the conduct is extreme and fatal. Although using an aggressive tone toward people when angry may indicate rudeness and arrogance, using hostile language or foul-mouthed words can incite actions that could lead to physical harm or attack. Prolonged anger does not have any benefits other than adding more physical and mental problems to our daily lives.

In a challenging environment and the face of unfair treatment, frustration can result in resentment. Resentment is a feeling of bitterness, especially about being treated unfairly or not being given rightful recognition. When individuals are treated unfairly or denied rightful recognition, they may develop feelings of resentment. Resentment might be experienced at the office, in family relationships, or other social situations. Resentment may deepen when there is a perceived downplaying or total disregard of someone's growth or accomplishments in a continual pattern. This can be demoralizing and disheartening.

Resentment can diminish motivation and reduce engagement, as it often manifests as passive-aggressive behavior that undermines individuals who feel mistreated or unappreciated. When this experience is prolonged, other negative emotions may combine with resentment to work together, which can affect communication, distort reasoning, and ruin friendships. Living with long-term resentment can take its toll on one's general mental well-being by sparking anxiety, worry, and even depression.

Feeling overwhelmed is another factor that may produce frustration. People who are overwhelmed can feel overpowered by the difficulties they encounter. They may feel exhausted and frustrated. These individuals may respond with outbursts of anger from growing suppressed emotions. They may also act aggressively to stop or manage perceived threats or injustices; frustration can trigger the fight-or-flight response. Poor Coping Mechanisms: If someone cannot find a way to regain power or control in an environment of stress, they might turn to violence as their method.

Aggression is the intense, often impermanent expression of frustration through words or actions designed to hurt others and impede one from accessing something desired (a goal). It occurs when someone is so fed up with a situation that they can't stand the insanity anymore and blows their top, hoping to at last free their demons.

There are three typical manifestations of aggression. *Verbal aggression*, which is the use of strong language when communicating or high-volume talk/yelling to assault someone in a pushy manner with anger verbally, is also a form of physical aggression. *Physical Aggression* is a way to act out frustration by slamming doors, punching objects, or, at worst, getting into altercations. Passive-aggressive behavior (sarcasm, intentional procrastination, and degradation) is an indirect expression of aggression arising from unaddressed irritation. One effect of aggressive behavior is broken relationships. Physical aggression can strain connections, creating fear and insecurity while hindering clear communication. In severe cases, it may lead to career-ending or legal consequences, particularly in professional or competitive settings.

Acting out in anger would increase the rage and guilt one feels from one's circumstances. In addition to frustration, a robust emotional response often includes powerlessness—the sense of being stuck and unable to do anything about it. Constantly struggling or confronting obstacles can be difficult for many reasons, draining us emotionally and hurting our overall well-being.

Reoccurring challenges are a common trigger of helplessness and frustration. For those who continue to face repeated setbacks or challenges where nothing appears to be working, it can feel like they are spinning their wheels. The idea is that the less control we have over our lives and situations, the angrier and more powerless we will feel.

For many, unresolved disputes or intractable problems—seemingly impossible to solve—can leave a feeling of failure lingering. Estimating an exorbitant maldevelopment is terrible for motivation. This means that everyone starts feeling helpless and out of their league because they cannot see what even the point of trying would do.

Repeatedly feeling powerless quickly fosters a fatalistic outlook on the future, making it nearly impossible for individuals to imagine changes of any kind or happy endings. Psychological Anxiety is when one feels helpless about being annoyed; it can lead to psychological pressures and then tension, extreme anxiety, and panic attacks, usually followed by sadness. Constant dissatisfaction can lead to a severe emotional state, where one is highly pessimistic about the future and feels lost hope. Depression can also lower a person's motivation and affect their overall mental health, especially in people who keep facing insurmountable hurdles or defeats.

It is tough to view the positive changes in one's life when it seems like nothing is improving for a while. If people face repeated difficulties in achieving their goals, especially if they consider them a measure of personal inadequacy, they may give up hope. Interpreting support from others as absent or waning in a time of need can turn minor difficulties into life-consuming battles where hope may only feel like an illusion.

People who have lost hope often lack motivation when they question their actions as not worth it or effective. Social withdrawal: People may isolate themselves from friends or family, leaving them hurt and thinking. Common Negative Cognitive Patterns: Hopeless People may develop negative cognitive patterns that cause them to be unable to see alternatives or sound options.

An apathetic, inattentive state of mind and heart often occurs after a long-term disappointment. If one faces perpetual setbacks or underperforms and decides not to care about them, one can become emotionally detached from one's pursuits. Recurring setbacks and disappointments can wreak havoc in someone's life and may ultimately halt the willingness to succeed. Someone who experiences setbacks or disappointment regularly may become apathetic and hold back their emotional reserves. One way people cope with feeling out of control is through apathy, where they detach emotionally and care less about what happens. Continual exposure to stressors or ongoing frustration contributes to burnout, where one feels emotionally exhausted and has little passion for participating in activities or goals.

The lack of motivation to complete specific tasks and the inertia of not wanting to do anything at all take a heavy toll on productivity. Emotional detachment can sabotage interpersonal connections because it's easy to conflate apathy with indifference or carelessness. Being unmotivated can also create a lousy image of ourselves by giving the impression that we are out of touch with what is essential goal-wise.

For someone seeking to work past their problems, it is of the utmost importance that we know how exactly these things trouble our emotions and put us in different emotional states. There are several key components to managing frustration more effectively: boosting emotional intelligence, practicing effective communication, and adopting healthy coping mechanisms. Acknowledging and dealing with these toxic emotions can help build resilience and enable a positive mindset in discouraging situations.

Chapter 2

The Nature of Human Emotional Energy

Emotional energy is the monsoon of feelings that can openly and secretly be granted to all your senses. The power or process of a person's mind can influence thoughts, actions, and overall well-being. This idea is founded on the notion that emotions affect more than just theoretically; they affect a person's physical state and well-being.

Positive emotions like happiness and excitement are believed to boost emotional energy, which enhances resilience and motivation, making it easier to recover from experiences and re-engage with the world. In contrast, negative emotions like anxiety or sadness can deplete emotional reserves and lead to emotional burnout or fatigue.

Energy and human emotion may be fundamentally different, but they share some symbolic properties, such as dynamic nature and transferability.

Energy in physics is a non-null quantity that moves energy needed for the universe's workings. Ultimately, it is defined by what you can do or change. Many different types of energy exist, with various characteristics and uses. Molecular kinetic energy derived from motion is an example of an object's life force/energy. In contrast, potential energy is stored capacity for action awaiting a trigger. Thermal energy is how we use heat to change the states of matter. The nature of energy is inherently dynamic since it changes from one form to another and influences the movements of physical systems while participating in the continuous evolution of the universe.

This dynamic, changing nature of human psychology is reflected in the emotions. Such states will evolve in response to both internal and external stimuli. Emotions are dynamic; they fluctuate in intensity and duration, manifesting as mild or overwhelming, fleeting or persistent. Emotions, like energy, strongly impact our thinking patterns, behavior, and interaction with others. So, for instance, the oratory of joy may compel us to spontaneous happy actions in a way that nuance of thought shapes more subdued responses. Like energy, emotions are an integral part of the rise and fall in our psychological landscape and contribute to the richness of human experience.

MASTERING FRUSTRATION

The Positive and negative states of human energy: Energy is also dual in physics or thermodynamics. Positive energy is the good energy that promotes positive change and better overall health in a system. For instance, renewable energy uses the positive aspects of nature to give power to our planet sustainably. On the other hand, negative energy can manifest itself in more destructive forms that create unrest or undesirable results. Another example of negative energy being potentially sinister is uncontrolled energy releases. You can see some of these releases in the environmental disasters.

While human emotions are subjective, whether positive or negative, they shape who we are. Positive emotions like joy, love, and contentment elevate and lift the human spirit, facilitating well-being while strengthening social connections. They enable good relational dynamics as well as self-fulfillment. Conversely, negative emotions like fear, grief, or anger represent complex parts of being human. These are complicated emotions to manage because they can interfere with individual growth and transfer onto others. However, negative emotions can force us to look deeper and improve, just like the reality of negative energy, which can also help bring a positive change.

The presence of both positive and negative states points towards a nuanced nature of these events regarding their energy and emotion. Whether an imbalance in physical reality or the complications of human psychology, these dualities demand our engagement to make and sustain positive outcomes across diverse domains.

Energy transfer is a fundamental concept in the dynamic stream of the physical universe observed in physics. Energy has the incredible ability to transfer between things and transform from one type to another without a hitch. We observe this transferability in day-to-day conditions, for example, when photosynthesis happens on Earth and the sun's radiant energy courses to the Earth or when electrical energy travels from an electrical source to gadgets to control them. Energy transfer is subject to fundamental principles that regulate the continuous exchange and transformation needed for any natural or engineered system.

Human emotion is a symbolic transfer of energy, rather than its generation or accumulation. Similarly, emotions are contagious in social settings—the mental state of one individual can spark a domino effect, influencing those they interact with. For example, a friend at a social function may be in high spirits and lift the spirits of others. Conversely, an isolated, gloomy idea or person could paint illusive and demoralizing pictures that drown people's souls. This idea of the transferability of emotions is a reminder that human beings are profoundly interrelated, and that one person's vibrations impact the emotional climate of a community.

Transferability suggests how intertwined (spatially, temporally, physically, and emotionally) systems are — both social and natural. These dynamics that transfer across events and situations are worth considering as we navigate the networked circumstances that impact our lived experiences.

The behavior of physical systems offers insight into physics, shedding light on how energy drives changes in behavior. The presence or absence of energy significantly influences the behavior of objects, including their interactions and ability to change. For instance, a car has kinetic energy as it needs the kinetic energy to move forward. If you consider potential due to a compressed spring, the amount of potential can define how this spring will behave once released. The activity of these physical objects is then intimately connected to the energy they contain, which determines how they move, what activities they perform, and how they respond to external stimuli.

Regarding human psychology, emotions also play an essential role in affecting behavior. Emotions—whether happiness, love, rage, or despair—play an important role in individuals' behavior.

Positive emotions often lead to open, social, and charitable behavior. However, destructive emotions trigger defensiveness and avoidance. Emotions significantly impact decision-making because people usually make decisions based on what they want to happen instead of logically weighing their options and making sound choices with rationality. The emotional climate can color affective relationships and influence cooperation, empathy, and communication between interpersonal relations.

The other fixture similarly etched under the physical and psychological systems is their impact on behavior. Understanding the influence of energy and emotion on human behavior provides insight into the natural world and human nature. These discoveries provide a holistic context for understanding the intricate interplay between external influences and behavioral responses.

Energy is contagious, a principle dictated by the laws of physics: when energy is concentrated in something, it spreads to nearby objects or systems, influencing them. The observation of this phenomenon is possible due to various forms of energy. For example, in the case of a vibrating guitar string, when this energy resonates across to other nearby strings on the instrument, it makes a pleasant sound and is infectious. Like that, energy propagates in space as electromagnetic waves and interacts with nearby objects en route. At the most fundamental level, the behavior of forces in our physical universe and their interdependent dance depends entirely on the contagious nature of energy.

Put differently, feelings are communicative in social and psychological contexts. There is a social aspect to emotion; a person in a group may catalyze emotion and influence others. A crowd can be energized by a common purpose, such as when someone speaks passionately. Conversely, a single person's stress or anxiety can permeate the emotional landscape and affect others. Experiences of sharing, whether positive or negative, create emotional resonance within a group, demonstrating the contagious nature of emotions.

However, emotions and energy are not analogous, so these analogies can only be understood to have a particular symbolic value that highlights common tendencies instead of exact similarities. Emotions occur on the complicated landscape of social dynamics and human psychology, while energy moves through the physical plane, obeying physical laws. This one senses these differences and does so to improve our understanding not of the world but instead of this tension between finite meanings of human experience interacting with actual physical forces.

The Spring Theory:

According to Spring Theory, human emotion can be modeled as a spring with three states: normal, compressed or stressful, and overstretched (frozen/disabled). This understanding compares spring's elasticity with the fluidity of feelings and showcases how balance and resilience are essential in emotions.

Standard State: When at rest, spring is typical, similar to the state where emotions are found when everything moves smoothly. By default, emotions are steady and balanced. This gives rise to a balance with which people may navigate the highs and lows of daily life with ease and mental clarity. Emotions are responsive in this state—appropriate, without excessive reactivity—to stimuli.

Compressed State: This theory states emotions can compress just like a spring. This is undergone by those who are stressed and distressed or have heightened emotional arousal. The compressed state can manifest itself as heightened tension, anxiety, or a sense of emotional pressure. If this compressed emotional state is not treated, it can be further squeezed and turned into a hard lump of iron, which may lead to emotional rigidity and psychological pressure.

Over-Stretched State: In contrast, feelings can extend beyond their limits, like a tightly coiled spring drawn past its breaking point. This is said to be the state of people who undergo prolonged hardship, excessive stress, or constant mental pressure. Overdoing it leads to exaggerated emotions, where one might struggle to cope with the hardship, resulting in heightened reactivity and emotional exhaustion.

If miscalibrated, the Spring Theory emphasizes the inherent risk and danger of compressed or overstretched emotional states. In the compressed mode, there is unchecked stress and emotional pressure, resulting in emotional breakdowns, burnout, or impaired decision-making. However, the stretched state can lead to emotional burnout, increased susceptibility to mental illness, and impact on personal relationships.

Striking a Balance:
This theory emphasizes the need for exercising some control over our emotions and not allowing them to become too closely squashed or expanded outwards from one another. It emphasizes the importance of cultivating emotional resilience and mindfulness—overcoming obstacles that cause emotions to shrink, while fostering their expansion through emotional regulation skills.

Spring Theory provides a symbolic framework that exemplifies the dynamic character of human emotions. The ability to notice and manage emotions is critical to continuing an adaptive response to the complexities of life and a general sense of well-being. Like a spring that only returns to order when not overly compressed or overstretched, emotions bring balance and resilience to the human experience when we can deal with them appropriately through knowledge and emotional resilience.

Chapter 3

The Spectrum of Our Emotional Energy

Emotional energy could be used metaphorically to refer to different types of energy when discussing how emotions can incite and influence the self and social relations. For example, people with high emotional energy may uplift or inspire others, but being surrounded by people with low emotional energy can do the reverse.

In brief, emotional energy is the vigor and strength gained from a person within their emotional life that affects various aspects of their life and experience with other people. Frustration signals that your feelings are trying to communicate something. Both verbal cues (like sarcasm) and nonverbal signals (such as sighs, body language, or venting) can convey emotional distress.

How we behave when frustrated depends on our emotions. Allowing ourselves to feel unhappy with something can be a coping mechanism, as it helps express our feelings to others. The response often depends on the level of frustration and the severity of the situation. It may result in anger, withdrawal, or resentment. It also guides us in choosing whether to resolve conflicts peacefully or remain silent.

Feelings affect the way people deal with one another. Negative complaints can strain relationships, while positive complaints can lead to understanding and assistance. Therefore, social support in times of distress may influence emotional well-being. The level of frustration a person experiences can influence their decision-making. This emotional bias in cognitive processes can cause individuals to make impulsive decisions or decide not to act. Understanding emotions helps in making conscious and equitable decisions.

There are only ten energy forms: Thermal energy, Electrical energy, Light energy, Radiant Energy, Sound energy, Motion or Kinetic Energy, Chemical Energy (potential), Mechanical energy(kinetic), and nuclear or gravitational. The way we process human emotions can be highly magical by accounting for different physical energies to understand our emotional world, which recognizes the similarities that energy has and how those imaginary worlds are handled in the minds of men. This conceptual model can benefit work-related frustrations, family crises, or individual prosperity struggles.

The following touches on the symbolic parallels between expressing our emotions and engaging with these energies.

Chemical energy—When we talk about human emotions, the emotional and physical force between two people is the chemical energy whose effect is felt on a metaphysical connection level. Consider the last time someone hugged you, whether it was your friend, family member, or partner. Hugs are not just about hugging; they represent good feelings. This is similar to the chemistry in the body and represents a non-physical connection encompassing interactions between emotions. In a passion scenario, a hug is simply a physical touch—a medium for an intense emotional connection that could cause one to trigger the other person's hormones and create bodily arousal in both parties.

When someone is hugging you, your brain releases chemicals and neurotransmitters, including oxytocin, the love hormone, or bonding hormone. The body releases these hormones, which can help facilitate a sense of emotional balance, safety, and comfort. This physical intimacy creates emotional closeness, and as we all know from experience, hugging your partner releases stamina-producing oxytocin, the love hormone.

Here, warmth is a tactile experience without physical touch, carrying the energy of exchange felt when being held. It serves as a brief moment of exposure, fostering love and bringing people closer. This illustrates how chemical energy fuels both our literal and metaphorical energy when interacting with others.

Mechanical: In humans, this often takes the form of physical labor. For instance, you are changing your body literally and metaphorically in the gym (the sequence of movements you perform) or on a specific exercise program (a sequential in-space pattern that utilizes our mechanical energy).

When you hit the gym, all that built-up energy in your muscles gets spent using chemical energy to convert it into mechanical work. This form of evolution plays out within the mind and heart. Endorphins are the feel-good hormones that your body releases when you challenge it physically to its limit.

It isn't only the physical movement of doing things and the state of being physically therapeutic, mentally and emotionally. A feeling of power may accompany it, or perhaps it could even feel exhilarating, coursing through your body like success. Exercise generates mechanical energy, a stimulant that helps boost good emotions like greater confidence and enhanced well-being.

MASTERING FRUSTRATION

Additionally, the drive and determination required to maintain an exercise routine bolsters one with mental strength and a more optimistic outlook. A symbolic connection between mechanical energy and vigor highlights the relationship between the body and mind, demonstrating how physical actions can directly influence mental and emotional conditions.

Nuclear emotion: An interpersonal analogy—atomic energy is metaphorically similar to the passion and vigor of spirited conversations or arguments. Such a vehement contention in which passions are high, and ideologies clash is identical to the fierce reaction in an atomic nucleus.

The nuclear reaction involves colliding and changing the atoms, releasing tremendous energy. Similarly, many ideas, opinions, and feelings clash when discussing or arguing. This collision generates emotional energy that manifests as intensity, passion, and excitement.

When you blow your top in an argument, it's less about the argument than the charge—the momentum created by your volley of force. The need to voice opinions, protest a cause, or seek affirmation may be motivated by palpable emotional energy. Like the energy released from a nuclear reaction, the raging emotional exchange during an argumentative discussion can be so cathartic that it expels repressed emotions and stimulates involvement and liveliness.

However, severe discussions can result in either understanding and resolution or the opposite of conflict, just like a nuclear reaction produces both good and bad results. Another analogy of atomic energy to a powerful emotional force suggests that good communication and constructive dialogue are the keys to unlocking the maximum potential for positive outcomes.

Relatable Gravitational Energy—The metaphorical emotional burdens of obligations and social and individual expectations can be compared to gravitational energy, the force of attraction between masses. Picture having a full plate of responsibilities and demands.

The weight of responsibility is the gravitational force of obligations and responsibilities one has in life, whether family, work, or different sorts of social jobs. Gravity represents the burden of these responsibilities and the sense of responsibility that accompanies them. It carries a real emotional burden, weighted according to the size of the responsibility.

Likewise, societal and self-expectations could weave an intangible puppet string about minimizing autonomous decisions. Growing

MASTERING FRUSTRATION

up, there is this gravitational pull to live up to or act out these expectations, which can change a person's life trajectory. The emotional experience of this gravitational energy is stress, the sense that you must (because, remember, gravity pulls in one direction only), and that constant feeling of needing to be reminded what others think of you.

Just as gravity keeps celestial entities in orbit around the proper suns, so do accountability, expectations, and other emotional forces hover like that over our lives. They metaphorically reflect the weight of responsibilities that take a toll on emotional health. This once again highlights the importance of balance and moderation, managing these gravitational pulls to maintain an enjoyable, functional life.

Light Energy: A common association with the initial spark of inspiration, creativity, and novelty—this can be attributed to light energy on a more human level. Consider epiphanies, flashes of insight, or ideas being born, like the light energy illuminating.

The "spark of creativity" is described in a way that parallels how light emerges from darkness, offering revelation and clarity. Like light that can interact with various surfaces to reveal alternative views, connecting disparate elements is often the essence of creativity. This union generates a bright energy that is illuminating and life-changing.

Inspiration flicks on a switch that casts out light and reveals new potentials and shadows left in darkness. Emotional light energy encompasses joyfulness, euphoria, and discovery excitement in this context. The feeling of a creative idea sparks your insides like a striking match.

Another exciting aspect of this allegoric relationship is that inspiration and light energy are enormously contagious. Creativity can spread, just like light can diffuse and fill a space. In a creative community, the give-and-take of ideas becomes a tangle of pictorial photons that scatter inspiration.

Using the metaphor of light energy and creative expression, this ultimately shows how one single spark can lead to something entirely new and beautiful, a creation process. (Madam Octopus Maxine Fortuna)

If I imagine it from the angle or view of human emotions, radiant energy can be that warm expression from within that makes one feel content and happy. It feels like a moment of pure joy, complete satisfaction, or peace, similar to the light that shines out of a bulb.

The "glow of happiness" is just a phrase indicating the happiness emitted from human feelings. Like light, happiness has a spreading quality. If someone is genuinely happy, they will vibrate their happiness, and uplift the people around them on an emotional level. With this emotional radiation, a positive energy emerges and creates bonds that generate happiness.

Using a figurative interpretation of rays of light and happiness, this signifies that good feelings originate from within. It's an inner lighthouse that shines brightly, unaffected by external conditions. Light energy vibrates through your entire body, creating a harmonious balance between thoughts, feelings, and experiences.

Additionally, the warmth of radiant energy also symbolizes comfort and protection gained through happiness. The emotional experience linked with radiant energy is satisfaction, gratefulness, and enjoyment of the moment. Like lying on the beach, the glow of joy makes one feel good and optimistically charged in life.

As a symbol of radiant energy, happy feelings and emotional contentment possess uplift transformation potential. It also demonstrates how an inner light can shine outward, affecting one's mood and those around them.

Sound Energy: Sound energy has metaphorically extended music's calmness and emotional resonation to cognitive functioning as a human experience. Consider how music can move through us, provoking visceral and sometimes cathartic responses.

The expression "therapeutic impacts of music" refers to the impact of sound energy through tunes and beats, which penetrate to the center levels of our feelings. Music, like sound waves that travel into our ears through the environment, reaches deep into our souls and makes us feel everything from joy to nostalgia, reflection, and peace.

We have long known the emotional power of sound energy, especially when it comes to silencing the mind. Music can change our way of feeling, giving relief when we are stressed and a voice when words fail us. Tone and rhythm create harmonious exchanges that speak a language much deeper than emotion.

The symbolic connection between sound in nature and sound energy in relation to emotional health underlines the therapeutic value of music. Just like a gentle breeze ruffles still waters, the soothing effect of music can relax, reduce stress, and provide an emotional outlet where one may ponder and heal.

In short, while sound's effect on our interior world is primarily symbolic, it shows the intimate relationship between sound energy and musical feeling. It highlights sound's role in shaping and influencing our emotions, as a powerful tool for self-reflection, communication, and emotional stability.

Motion Energy—The emotional experiences of exploration and play can translate figuratively to motion energy in the human realm. With the new moon, consider your own space travel, real ticket sales, new endeavors, first-time experiences, or even adopting fresh paradigms.

The term 'Thrill of adventure' embodies the dynamic nature of motion energy. Movement can be literal or metaphorical, and nearly everyone is aware of the boost one feels and could benefit from. Anything in motion enjoys kinetic energy. New relationships, new places to go, or new ideas to explore all become sources of emotional fuel.

Movement energy is also the thrilling combination of even more fun: stepping outside your comfort zone and learning more about yourself. And that means embracing change and everything it entails. The symbolic link between kinetic energy and being on the verge of new worlds speaks to how experiences that propel us forward can be transformative, expanding who we are and adding dimensions to our knowledge.

Motion energy is the act of moving, but how we influence the world (not just physically) is more than that: it also includes the momentum of personal growth and self-discovery. Someone who is rolling towards their goals, objectives, and aspirations is not only happy but also feels like a ball.

Therefore, we find a metaphorical relationship between the energy of motion and the yearning for adventure and exploration, thereby highlighting the dynamic and transformational role that movement plays in our lives. It points to the joy that comes in embracing movement, change, and that endless journey of self-exploration.

Thermal energy: The human connections that we find most comforting and endearing can be approximated by what is called thermal energy in the domain of human emotions. The feel of a warm hand on yours, the warmth from a deep embrace, or the heat from an authentic smile are symbolically represented as heat energy.

The warmth of a gesture reflects how the depth of compassion, understanding, and empathy with which it is delivered also carries its own impact. Just as thermal energy is associated with the motion of heat, during human interactions, happy feelings that give solace and alleviation are exchanged to develop emotive warmth (Pavlović, 2023).

Some things, as simple as a handshake or even a pat on the back, can comfort people by letting them know they are safe and feel heard. Likewise, a genuine smile may portray warmth and express care. These cathartic exchanges create a new kind of warmth that wraps around individuals metaphorically, providing them with crucial emotional shelter and sustenance.

Thermal energy relates to the emotions of reassurance, comfort, and being taken care of. It highlights how warmth underlies emotional health and the nourishing cocoon of pleasant relationships.

Furthermore, the symbolic transfer of thermal energy in gestures like consolation supports the idea that emotions can be transmitted and communicated similarly to heat. Genuine caring and kindness snowballs warmth outwards to create an emotionally happy climate.

Simply put, it reinforces the boundaries of our human existence, transcending divisions and highlighting the power of emotional warmth in personal relationships. It emphasizes the importance of compassion, empathy, and positivity in creating a soothing and nurturing emotional environment.

Electrical Energy: In terms of human emotions, electrical energy metaphorically represents moments of pure desire, excitement, or anticipation. Like electricity, it pulses through us in the exhilaration of starting something new, a feeling that builds before a significant event or the gamble of embarking on an adventure.

"This jolt of excitement" embodies the idea that electrical energy is active and dynamic. Just as electricity powers a device, interest has a similar energizing effect on humans. This burst of energy is often accompanied by a heightened sense of awareness, excitement, and anticipation for what lies ahead.

The electrifying feeling: the thrill of some uncertainty, the joyous expectation, and the sweet pressure that builds before all significant moments. This flood of excitement serves as a trigger, pushing individuals to chase after their passions, take risks, and explore new possibilities like the spark that ignites a current.

The connection perceived here, too, between the electrical energy quenched and the emotional experience, like the excitement of the excited emotion, reflects that positive emotions transform and inspire us. The enthusiasm sparks human-driven work and creativity that aims to lead people to creative results, similar to an electric current that powers a system.

In short, the analogy between electrical current and the emotions of anticipation and excitement reinforces how much more kinetic and passion-fueled these feeling energies are in our lives. Employing optimistic expectations can kindle our aspirations, add a splash of zest, and light up a spark.

These examples show how human emotion and behavior might correspond figuratively with various energy sources. We hope to showcase the multi-dimensionality of these relationships by providing instances where emotions correlate with different energy modes. Such a study highlights the multifaceted nature of human experience and the constant interplay between emotions and the psychosocial energy they trigger.

MASTERING FRUSTRATION

Chapter 4

Types of Frustration and Stressors

Everyone has felt irritation in their lives—the feeling that some onion gets lodged, things are not going as planned, or their expectations are shattered. Sadness is a common human experience and ubiquitous across all spectrums of existence. It is perhaps used to describe times when we think our efforts have reached their culmination and results are less than expected.

Frustration takes many forms, and to successfully deal with its challenges, we must identify these various types. Let's examine the kinds of irritation to help you focus your conversation on an individual type. By reviewing specific situations, we can foster awareness of the complexity behind frustration and develop strategies to deal with its intricacies.

Here are six of the most common human frustrations. Each has its respective triggers and effects. Identifying and classifying these types is the first step to successful frustration management, if not mitigation, in your life. We will discuss each type in the following sections and provide tactics and tips on navigating the tangle of frustration from the storm fractals of their context.

1. Interpersonal Frustration

Interpersonal frustration stems from our relationships with others. It can occur in friendships, family, and even professional relationships. Expectations—our own or other people's—can often lead to discontent and frustration.

Your best friend said they would help you with a project but kept flaking on you. This frustration arises out of expectations that have not been met in the context of friendship.

Everybody experiences interpersonal frustration. It comes from the people we deal with—family members, friends, and workmates. This often occurs when our expectations of these relationships do not match reality. To understand this frustration, let us look at some relatable instances.

Getting stuck in family relationships can be particularly difficult. Imagine a situation where you have arranged for a long-awaited family trip. You look forward to some good time, rest, and peace. But what happens is that many times, the opposite occurs. Frustration can also be caused by sibling bickering, complaints about what to do, or interruptions. Interpersonal frustration may come quickly because of the natural contrast between your expectations vs. what happens in real-time family dynamics.

Keeping close friendships is also based on reliability and trustworthiness. It can get annoying if a friend repeatedly promises assistance working on a project but does nothing. It shows the difference between what we expect them to be and that they never even tried.

Interpersonal frustration is not limited to intimate relationships. A far more common context is that it tends to sneak into the workplace. Consider being part of a team that thrives on collaboration. Frustration can surface if your co-workers do not seem to communicate, creating misunderstandings and disruptions. You envision a seamless partnership, yet the opposite is true.

Some techniques can make resolving conflict among employees at the workplace a game-changer. In personal relationships, a little less expectation and a touch of understanding of the other perspective can go a long way. Here's the thing—when we become aware of our frustration as it's triggered, we are faced with a two-sided choice.

    2. Workplace Frustration:

MASTERING FRUSTRATION

Workplace frustration originates from the pressure and demands of our job and significantly affects both professional and personal life. To address this type of frustration, consider the use cases below.

Long working hours are a prevalent reason for workplace frustration. When your job takes too much time and energy, it can cause you to become burned out. You may come into the office consistently late, sacrificing your time and feeling burnt out. Your expectations of a work-life balance compared to the reality of fucking your entire life away at the office could serve as fodder for frustration.

Apart from this, unrealistic expectations of superiors or management also lead to workplace frustration. Consider the possibility that, whenever you are told to do something with a timeline or associated turnover time, your boss has instructed you to deliver in an unrealistic time frame. That difference between your human ability to achieve and what's asked of you is a significant source of stress and dissent.

If a team does not communicate effectively, it breeds confusion and irritation. If the team members do not openly communicate, give vague commands, or indulge in tussles, it hampers the work process. You expect to work together seamlessly; instead, you may find that they over-communicate or never communicate, and constant bickering ensues, turning into mutual annoyance.

Boundaries often need to be set to overcome workplace frustration, and clear communication is essential—an art that so many leaders seem entirely out of touch with. If long hours burn you out, discussing workload and work-life balance with management is essential. If someone has unrealistic expectations, honestly communicating your workload and capacity can help alleviate frustration. In the workplace, where we need to communicate well and resolve conflicts quickly, team settings can help promote this.

By understanding workplace frustration and taking steps to alleviate it, one can create a more rewarding work experience with less stress. Find the sweet spot between what you want from your work and what is possible so that your professional life adds to your growth rather than maximizing frustration.

3. Financial Frustration:

Financial fear is one of the most common sources of frustration many face throughout their life. Typically, it relates to an inability to make ends meet or the sense that you are not where you should be financially. This emotional gap is often fertile ground for the distance between what you expect to bring financially and your situation's reality. When your monthly bills exceed your income, and you cannot save or achieve financial objectives, you may feel frustrated financially. It is time to dive deeper into this type of frustration using some relatable examples.

One common cause of money problems is the bills you have on a month-to-month basis—your rent or mortgage, utilities, insurance, and other life expenses exceed what you make every month. But this money gap can make you hard-working and even feel helpless. You would have thought all that financial stability was a good thing, but it turns out it's more of a stretched financial balancing act.

Student Loan Debt is something that causes financial frustration for many humans. Waking up to a mammoth student debt after all these years can be overwhelming, especially when you've finally reached the point where you can pursue your lifelong dream—earning a high salary, living independently, eating well, and enjoying the luxury of traveling. The truth, however, comes with a crushing load of debt that could have you struggling to make the monthly payments.

Money goals like home ownership, children, and retirement can be frustrating when they seem out of reach. You assume you will be on course with your financial goals; however, the truth is usually different because of unforeseen expenses or capital difficulties.

MASTERING FRUSTRATION

To manage money frustrations, you need financial literacy and budgeting skills. Be sure to establish an achievable budget based on your income and expenses. If you're in debt, either student loans or credit card debt, you'll need more money to reach your bank account with a financial plan and steady repayments.

Moreover, seeking the help of a financial expert or taking a financial education class will equip you with various ideas and tips that can lessen your financial stress. By improving your finances, you can work towards a less frustrating and discombobulated economic future.

4. Time Management Frustration:

Time management frustration is driven by a lack of time to complete tasks or feeling overwhelmed. We have all experienced the clock running out on us and our task list growing.

Say a student has to balance classes, work part-time, and be active in extracurriculars. They could find this overwhelming. There is a short time for studies and personal life, which may cause even more frustration.

Another common type of frustration that you could experience either in your daily work or related fields, even outside the job, is time management frustration. Usually, it comes from not having enough time to complete your task or feeling overwhelmed by what lies ahead of you. We can understand this kind of frustration with some examples.

Doesn't it feel like work, family, and personal life tend to throw time management out the window for most? You should be able to use your time wisely, but instead, you run from one thing to the next, skip family functions, and rarely have a moment for yourself.

When you have to meet more than one deadline in your work or school life, it can be frustrating from a time management standpoint. You think you will master your time management, but it can mean a hectic timetable filled with sleepless nights and endless stress.

The second most common source of frustration in managing time is the dreaded to-do list. While you plan to get through everything systematically, your to-do list accumulates undone chores, creating a disorder.

To manage time efficiently, we must establish priorities, set obvious objectives, and have fixed norms. Learning to say no and delegate some of your responsibilities can help ease the frustration around time management issues. You can always use time management techniques, such as the Pomodoro or time blocking, to regain control of your schedule and avoid frustration.

Overcoming frustration with time management will help you live a more organized, balanced life that allows for work-life-family and self-care balance. We all need time for ourselves.

5. Internal Frustration:

Internal frustration is like an emotional battle you're waging with yourself. This tendency toward perfectionism is often rooted in an illusion, temporary low self-esteem, or the weight of self-imposed burdens.

Take perfectionists who hold themselves to impossible standards. They will feel disappointed in themselves and may even doubt their self-worth because they simply could not meet these standards.

Frustration is one of the most exciting types because it causes you to be at war with yourself. It is usually born out of impossibly high expectations, a complete lack of self-belief, or being crushed under the weight of expectations one has imposed on oneself. Now, let's explore this form of frustration with some real-life scenarios.

Not doing things perfectly is frustrating in itself. You hold yourself to an unrealistic standard, where anything less than perfect is unsubstantial. However, life is imperfect, and this leads to frustration and self-doubt.

Negative self-talk and constantly criticizing yourself can also lead to internal frustration. You would think you would keep a positive self-image, but the reality is continuous self-deprecation.

Tip: Internal frustration could stem from too much self-imposed pressure to be at your best in every area of life. We anticipate effortlessly juggling work, relationships, and personal growth, all while impostor syndrome and burnout lurk just around the corner.

Fighting internal annoyance can only come with kindness and awareness. Unrealistic expectations should be suspended, and self-tormenting thought patterns must be replaced with positive affirmations. Trained therapy or self-help sources can be desirable aids to managing anger inside.

On the positive side, of course, nurturing a good relationship with yourself and accepting that being human is imperfect can relax some of that inner frustration and help you see yourself in a better light.

6. External Frustration:

Another type of frustration is external frustration, which stems from events in your life you cannot control. That possibility can entail everything from a traffic jam, the weather not cooperating, an unexpected illness, or other unforeseen occurrences. This is how we respond to things beyond our control.

Picture yourself sitting in a lengthy backup en route to a critical meeting. This situation can also lead to frustration because you cannot change the outside event.

Traffic jams during your daily commute are a well-known source of external frustration. You anticipate riding to work with ease, but instead, you have gridlocked visitors, and your temper turns angry and stressed.

Nobody plans around the weather, but sometimes, when your plans get messed up due to rain or stormy conditions, it can create quite a bit of frustration. You think you will be outside in the sunshine, but it rains, and now what do you do? Cancel or move things around?

The slammed door of an external aggravation involving your health often takes the form of immediate sickness or injury to you or someone you care about. You plan on being healthy, and as it turns out, that can mean dealing with the anxiety associated with your unexpected health problems as well.

An external sense of frustration indicates that you may need a period of rest or self-care to regain balance. Although you have no power over external events, you do have control of your reaction to those events. Practicing stress-relief strategies (like deep breathing or mindfulness) will allow you to cope with the frustration of outside sources. So, have backup plans for your activities and practice patience in aggravating predicaments to minimize the stress of frustrating things occurring beyond the self.

For traffic jams and commuting woes, please plan your commute with buffer time in mind. This helps you understand possible delays and alleviates the stress of unanticipated traffic. In case you are stuck in a jam, listening to audiobooks/podcasts or soothing music on your way can reduce frustration and increase enjoyment as well.

Consider having backup indoor plans for your events that the weather may disrupt. It is imperative to remain flexible and adapt to changes in weather. You may find that a rainy day can sometimes be great for hanging indoors or prospecting a good book.

MASTERING FRUSTRATION

Health-related setbacks cut the deepest here; you often cannot help it, and dealing with that frustration proves even more complex than the endeavor itself. You must consult a medical professional and seek support to overcome health issues. Staying positive and being grateful for your health will make these external irritations easier.

Accepting that external annoyances are part of existence and cannot be eliminated is critical in handling this frustration. With these skills, you can handle what life throws at you with greater ease and lessen the damage those things can do to your happiness.

But frustration is a complicated emotion and takes multiple types. Frustration comes in various forms, from interpersonal, workplace, and financial frustration to time management and internal and external frustration. The equal variety comes with its individual set off and needs unique responses to crack. Recognizing and owning these frustrations creates space to live a more balanced life. Frustration is a common human experience, and if you have the right tools and techniques, the storms of your frustration can be weathered resiliently and gracefully.

MASTERING FRUSTRATION

Chapter 5

The Telltale Signs of Frustration

Frustration rarely creeps in without kicking up some dust about a mile back. Like the calm before a rainstorm, some cues appear before frustration hits. These can be both nuanced and overt signals, but they will always present you a chance to step in before the frustration has set in completely.

But be on the lookout for these commonplace in-flight warning signs.

Overwhelm is more than just frustration; it's an emotion that feels like you're drowning in it. It occurs when frustration escalates to a tidal ferocity, flooding your mental space and leaving you to survive solely by exerting sheer willpower, relying on your mental strength to navigate through. It can be triggered by taking on too much, feeling powerless against systemic forces, or facing a crisis.

Overwhelming arises when people try to do too much at once and feel the stress of being pulled in every direction. Work, family, personal time, and social obligations piled up can create a pressure cooker of too many things to manage, and that eventually gets overwhelming. The burden of these roles becomes a tsunami pulling so forcefully that the ability to function will be washed away.

One of the things that can cause us to feel overwhelmed is a sustained sense of helplessness. Frustration is further compounded into a raging torrent that drowns rational thought and the ability to cope when people feel challenges are enormous or they cannot act or change. The feeling that you cannot help and that some things feel out of control brings a wave of emotion.

When a crisis strikes—be it personal, professional, or societal—it often comes without warning, leaving us feeling overwhelmed. When the challenge or unexpected event is so immense that it sparks intense frustration, it's as though the sculpture of our resilience is inundated with too much sand. In moments like these, the emotional tide rushes in, threatening to drown out rational thought and hinder our ability to adapt.

When one is overwhelmed, he/she/they may end up having all sorts of reactions (emotionally and physically) to that situation. Such can be increased anxiety, inability to focus, a feeling of 'brain freeze,' and a sense of losing access to one's familiar coping strategies.

MASTERING FRUSTRATION

Our breath changes when we are frustrated. It can become faster and more shallow to match the intense emotion of the moment. The physiological stress response of frustration has a similar effect where you feel your heart pounding in your chest.

This change in how you breathe is a way in which frustration can manifest itself, and it might be more recognizable as emotional intensity rises. In real-time, the body reacts to the stressor and instinctively modifies its breathing pattern based on what is required. Breath is rapid and shallow—a physical manifestation of what is brewing within, mirroring the quickening cadence of thought and feeling.

Frustration can also cause an accelerated heart rate. With the body operating at an increased level of excitement, the breath and heartbeat exist in a close dance that is very much felt. There is a pounding in the chest, a physical feeling of heartbeats speeding through the body, signaling tension and stress.

This physiological response is hardwired into our body as a by-product of the evolution of its mechanisms to respond to all signs of danger. The fight-or-flight response, triggered by stressful situations, puts the body on high alert. When faced with a similar scenario, your body instinctively prepares to fight, flee, or freeze—even if these reactions manifest mentally or emotionally.

If you are annoyed, avoid eye contact. Legal life increases the risk of confrontation or vulnerability, and to protect against that, one uses legal status privilege.

Avoiding eye contact during moments of frustration is often a subconscious instinct to create a mental barrier. Returning their gaze may reveal a silent request for a brief reprieve—an opportunity to build an emotional shield to process their thoughts and feelings without the risk of immediate confrontation. It's as though averting their eyes offers a temporary escape from the weight of the situation, granting them a moment to regroup and reset.

Also, not looking someone in the eye helps to protect yourself. The eyes are the window to the soul; they often convey emotions that our words cannot. During moments of frustration, people may want to keep these emotional indicators hidden; they prefer (and deserve) privacy from others in the nature and sense of their internal environment. This intentional act of turning our back serves as a protective measure, safeguarding the tenderness that comes with passion.

MASTERING FRUSTRATION

In addition, refusing to make eye contact is a form of boundary communication. It lets other people know that this person is not ready to be engaged at this time; it creates a physical and emotional barrier between one another. An implicit request for some air under the space when it comes to air, without saying precisely that.

More broadly, this behavior is a cultural norm and personality trait. In certain cultures, direct eye contact is a prime indication of transparency and honesty, while in other cultures, it can be seen as intimidating if sustained. Of course, personal preferences and comfort levels also affect how people deal with eye contact when frustrated.

The more nuanced explanation for why we avoid eye contact when frustrated lies in self-preservation—it's a way to shield ourselves from confrontation while offering a glimpse of vulnerability without fully exposing it. This subtle, nonverbal cue also signals a need for space, a classic gesture in human communication. Understanding this aspect of behavior can help cultivate patience and foster more empathetic, effective communication in social and interpersonal interactions.

Furrowing the brow provides visual evidence even more visceral than numbers or spreadsheets of the tumult that frustration can trigger in times like this—where emotions and physical experience intersect deeply. The movement of the muscles above the eyes during moments of frustration, anger, or annoyance serves as a visible signal to others of your emotional state. This muscle contraction forces the skin to crease, forming distinctive lines between the eyebrows that communicate displeasure or irritation.

This brow furrowing goes beyond a mere show; it embodies how one feels inside on those less illustrious occasions when exasperation threatens to overwhelm. Those deep lines carved across the forehead emotionally cause it to broadcast loudly. The knitted brow is an exterior manifestation of the contour of thoughts and feelings on the inside.

The physiological reason for this furrowing goes deep into the body, and it causes this instinctive reaction during times of stress and conflict. Faced with ever-increasing frustration, the body prepares for action, and frowning eyebrows subtly reveal this readiness. The face is the canvas on which an emotional narrative is painted, and the furrowed brow is a brushstroke.

The act of furrowing the brow is not simply physical but has cultural and social meaning. It has been heralded as a universally noted sign of disgust, annoyance, or a clash within. It silently delivers a message—an outward manifestation of an internal struggle.

By understanding that the frown is an external manifestation of internal stress, we see the inextricable relationship between mind and body. It also recalls the subtle variations of how emotions can express themselves bodily, offering those witnessing some insight into an individual's emotional experience. Additionally, for the person feeling frustrated, noticing these physical sensations can trigger them to bring awareness to themselves and make a conscious effort to deal with the emotion accompanying it.

The most frequently recognized symptom of frustration is irritability. You react more quickly or impatiently to things that may not usually bother you. Perhaps you will sit tapping your foot or sighing and checking your watch. The sighing reply of too much would put us in frustration mode. It is how your body tells you it is overwhelmed and needs to release the tension. Understanding the early stages of frustration is essential in navigating these complex signals. If you can nip that frustration in the bud, it is much less likely to develop into a giant emotional blow-up and will be easier to handle.

Feeling tense in the body is another sign. Be aware if you are clenching your muscles, like in your shoulders, neck, or jaw. You may be unknowingly clenching out of frustration. That indicates the pressure is coming, which means you are trying to constrict on dumping how you feel. You clench the jaw when you are annoyed. Otherwise, it can result in jaw pain as well as migraines. This allows you to either stop this frustration from spiraling into a significant emotional disturbance or handle it better.

Because they become frustrated and then irritated, this is the next step. Once irritation escalates, you may become irritable, easily angered by minor inconveniences, or even agitated by the slightest annoyance. When frustrated, your body may instinctively display defensive or aggressive signals. This can include folding your arms, adopting a guarded stance, or using exaggerated gestures to express your frustration. These behaviors often serve as a physical outlet for emotional tension, visibly communicating your inner state. You express most of it with your body language while trying to make your point.

Clenched fists are another visible sign of frustration—like your body is getting ready for a battle that isn't there. The disappointment is so great at times that it surfaces as yelling or screaming—a vocal release that could only be described as pure vexation.

MASTERING FRUSTRATION

One of the surest indications that frustration is even tempting is that it happens to everything going on inside our heads. The mind may wander from the task, stray into where the frustration comes from, or be inundated with thoughts of unworthy pricing output. That drift in thought indicates the agitation that frustration introduces to cognition, distracting individuals from what they are doing and diffusing mental effort across multiple paths.

Frustration can make the mind more open to distractions from the outside world. In this state of increased emotional activity, one is more likely to be distracted by external stimuli. Under typical situations, it might be a slight annoyance, but when frustration is setting in, it can become a massive diversion. This additional distractibility makes it even harder to stay on task.

When someone feels frustrated, the most apparent is the cry for help to focus and concentrate. Pulling the focus into frustration can have a staggering impact on your capacity to be fully present with what you are doing. The cognitive environment transforms, and many struggle to remain focused.

It turns out that one of the variables in this is cognitive appraisal. Cognitive appraisal is a critical construct in the investigation of stress, emotion regulation, and resilience. Such an awareness of contextual assessment is helpful to emotional intelligence, allowing individuals to respond adaptively not only to challenges and stressors but also, ultimately, to their interactions around their lives.

An individual would conduct a cognitive appraisal, which means assessing events, situations, or experiences based on their beliefs and dreams. This evaluation of mental functioning is integral to emotional and behavioral responses to just about anything. An experience is just an experience until we add emotional weight to it by way of interpretation, and interpretation determines action.

The two most common kinds of cognitive appraisal are Primary Appraisal and Secondary Appraisal. The first stage, Primary Appraisal, involves an individual assessing whether an event holds significant implications. This evaluation happens quickly, almost unconsciously, as the experience is stripped of its deeper meaning and context. It is then categorized as irrelevant, benign/positive, or negative and potentially threatening. How we feel about the situation depends on this appraisal. After something is considered to be potentially relevant or threatening in the primary appraisal, a further evaluation happens. Following this, the next phase is Secondary Appraisal, which evaluates one's ability to cope with or manage the demands posed by a given dangerous situation. This takes into account things like your personal resources available, skills that you have, and how much the person believes they can control the situation. The result of secondary appraisal subsequently determines the emotional response and behavioral tendencies.

The cognitive appraisal process is decidedly subjective by nature, as each individual brings their own perspective, beliefs, and previous experiences to the interpretation of a situation. This individuality means that even when faced with the same event, two people may appraise it in entirely different ways based on their distinct cognitive frameworks. Appraisal processes are essential in determining the emotional value assigned to an event. A positive appraisal can elicit emotions such as joy or happiness, while a negative appraisal will generate fear, anger, and sadness.

Cognitive appraisal strongly tempers the selection of coping strategies and behavioral responses. When people appraise situations adaptively, effective problem-solving and positive coping often follow, whereas maladaptive appraisals commonly lead to avoidance, emotional dysregulation, or other maladaptive aspects of coping strategies. Appraisals influence the processes that lead to decision-making. Because appraisals can influence coping choices and actions, the appraisal process plays a vital role in how individuals choose to act when faced with a situation.

Now emotions, as it turns out, are closely linked to cognitive appraisal. Simply put, there are going to be times when we will fail in life, and this goes hand-in-hand when people assess or evaluate the current state of affairs and their ability (or lack thereof) to overcome hurdles when they face them. Negative appraisals may heighten frustration and negative emotions, whereas a positive appraisal causes a more adaptive response. This influence extends to the kind of cognitive appraisal that is made (i.e., threat vs. challenge) and specific strategies that are selected in response to stressors. A challenge appraisal of a situation may elicit an approach to coping style, whereas threat appraisal may evoke avoidance or defensive coping. Cognitive appraisals are part of global subjective well-being. Unfavorable evaluations can affect life satisfaction, and continued poor appraisals may lead to stress, anxiety, or depression.

As it turns out, frustration is a cognitively heavy experience that does more than distract. Frustration, in particular, is an intensely emotionally charged concept that can hinder cognition by inhibiting our capacity to make optimal decisions and solve problems. Things that usually would be easy with a clearer mind become hard work, as there is much emotional chaos to deal with in the mind.

MASTERING FRUSTRATION

If you know more about these cognitive shifts, you will be able to formulate functional strategies to help when frustration arises. Integrating mindfulness strategies, like grounding exercises or short mental breaks, into your routine may allow you to reset focus and bring attention back to the task. A less distracting and more appropriate work environment can also aid in gaining focus.

The relationship between frustration and cognitive attention is complex and multifaceted. Understanding that frustration can cloud the mind's ability to focus makes it clear that purposeful intervention is necessary, which builds resilience and increases the ability to deal with challenges more clearly.

How do you see what happens after frustration? By becoming an observer of yourself. Notice how frustration shows up in your body and mind and how you relate to others. In doing so, you emphasize an essential part of your frustration mastery process.

To kick-start these efforts, try this exercise:
When looking back on your day, think about how you felt. Do you ever find it frustrating? How are they impacting your mood and health?

Observe physical sensations associated with frustration. Does tension, a pounding heart, or discomfort come out? Document what occurs with these sensations to better understand the mind/body relationship.

Watch how you interact with others while being frustrated. Are there conflicts or miscommunications that seem to be associated with your emotional state?

Monitor your frustration level and its effect on your daily activities. Are you more productive when angry, or does that hinder your work?

This is a perfect moment for some introspection. Think back to the last time you experienced frustration. What were the early warning signs for you? Think about when you became overwhelmed with frustration and what you did or how you could have reacted differently.

Being aware of these signs is your way to equip yourself with the means to cope with frustration. The more you practice this, the better prepared you will be to face life with some degree of poise and strong determination.

Chapter 6

The Price of Frustration

If left unchecked, frustration taxes your psyche and exacts a heavy toll on your mental, emotional, and physical health. Here is a tip: frustration does not exist in a vacuum; it is part of an intricate interplay of emotion and behavior.

When frustration ensues, it creates a domino effect, setting out ripples that leave no stone unturned, impacting every scope of wellness. These are subtle or glaring but significant.

Now, let us explore a few of these hidden costs:
Frustration takes a toll on the emotional battery. It can make us tired, cranky, and overwhelmed, and we cannot be present in the joyous moments of our lives. Frustrations are energy suckers and kill enthusiasm. This results in lower productivity and motivation, making it harder to overcome whatever is causing the feelings of frustration. Frustration lowers productivity and often results in additional errors. That can relate to your job and keep you from growing in your career and being satisfied.

Anger is a common reaction to frustration, but when it lingers for an extended period, it can take a toll on mental and physical health. Prolonged anger is associated with elevated stress levels, an increased risk of heart problems, and weakened immunity. At its peak, unresolved anger can significantly impact overall well-being. But frustration has an impact that is more than emotional. This evolves into stress that does show up in our body: tension, headaches, digestive issues, and eventually severe health conditions.

If you do not know how to deal with frustration, you may make wrong decisions and act impulsively. Frustration can cloud our ability to reason or make good decisions. This will result in acting impulsively and deciding on something we may regret later.

When frustration is chronic, it can create learned helplessness and hopelessness about finding relief. Wallowing in a cycle of failure can cut too close for bone comfort and get ugly and highly nasty.

Concentrating and focusing are difficult when frustration is ever-present. This may lead to reduced productivity and performance.

MASTERING FRUSTRATION

Frustration makes you emotionless toward others. It may cause you to isolate yourself from socialization, making you feel lonely.

A sense of emptiness and discontentment often breeds tension, which can directly impact our mental and emotional well-being. Stress is a natural consequence of frustration, and chronic stress is a significant factor behind many physical conditions, such as high blood pressure, gastrointestinal issues, difficulty sleeping, and decreased immunity. Eventually, it can lead to more significant health problems.

Because of the emotional distress induced by frustration, some people resort to unhealthy behaviors like abusing psychoactive substances. This can only fuel addiction and mental issues.

Frustration can create significant challenges in both personal and professional relationships. Unchecked frustration can seep into conversations, leading to misunderstandings, conflicts, and tension in both private and workplace interactions. This can leave you feeling isolated and disconnected from others.

Depression and anxiety can be brought on by frustration. Chronic frustration may help to precipitate depression and anxiety disorders. And thus, the vicious cycle continues, as these conditions only serve to intensify frustration.

Accepting and understanding the risks of childhood trauma in our lives which remain with us into adulthood is one thing; learning healthy coping strategies, communication skills, and emotional regulation techniques is another matter everyone faces. This will keep your brain and body safe from thought-provoking ideas that can take you on a downward spiral of such negative feelings, even when you do not want to experience any event because it intervenes in your daily life so much, so protect both by doing the right thing.

Acknowledge the Emotional Drain:
1. How frequently do you get frustrated, and what areas of your life are more prone to it?
2. What feelings come up with your frustration? Do you frequently encounter anxiety, rage, or despair?
3. When you feel frustrated, do you experience physical symptoms such as muscle tension, headaches, or sleep problems?
4. Think about how frustration has impacted your relationships. Has that caused you some disagreements or disengagement, too?

The moment you realize the price of that frustration is a defining point in your rise toward mastery. It is a solid incentive to shift into action and do the work necessary to rewire and transmute frustration.

MASTERING FRUSTRATION

Chapter 7

Battling with Inner Demons

It is commonly said that fighting your inner demons means dealing with possible internal conflict—facing the enemy known as yourself. This metaphor conveys the intimate fight.

Maya was a young professional who wanted to work on self-improvement for better well-being. She wished to tune up facets of her life for betterment—health, work-life balance, etc. But despite starting this entire process of metamorphosing, she faced quite an internal tug-of-war—a war of her own emotions.

Maya pledged to get in shape, which included exercising more and balancing her diet. At the same time, she hoped to establish better boundaries at work that would lead to a more sustainable balance between her professional and personal life. Yet, as Maya sought to go more deeply into these shifts, she became frustrated with herself.

The emotional game was constructed when it came to breaking the old and getting into a new routine. Her need for instant gratification made her impatient, leading to insecurity, frustration, and doubt. However, the flip side is that being open to improving requires tough skin and determination—often making the internal struggle even stronger. Her inner battle highlighted the importance of self-compassion, patience, and celebrating small victories along the way.

The example is how death by a million internal cuts can be an essential ugly part of the journey. This internal struggle to become a better version of oneself means that you need to be more challenging and realistic about gradual change within yourself that is transformational. This story of Maya tells us that working on improving oneself without recognizing, acknowledging, and addressing internal frustrations can lead to short-lived positive outcomes.

Below are methods for dealing with and working through these internal difficulties:

It starts with being conscious of yourself. Recognize and recognize the thoughts, feelings, or behavioral patterns that are causing your inner conflicts. This is an essential first step in understanding what causes the problems.

Practice mindfulness daily. Seeing your thoughts without judgment enables you to understand better what happens in your inner landscape. Many techniques can help, but meditation and deep breathing might well be the ones you need.

Call out negative and self-sabotaging thoughts. Doubt their certainty and let them play second fiddle to more empowering alternatives. Cognitive-behavioral therapy (CBT) techniques can be instrumental here.

This is not equivalent to going on a diet, so if your inner demons seem impossible to defeat, ask for help. Therapists and counselors can offer guidance, tools, and safe space to help work through internal battles.

Look for that safe surrounding within the family or trust circle. Talk to trustworthy people who can offer empathy, encouragement, and guidance.

Set realistic and attainable goals. Do not overwhelm yourself with the more significant challenges; take one step at a time. Acknowledge critical milestones to celebrate progress and help create a feeling of success.

Practice habits that promote good health and wellness. Exercise and nutrition are paramount for health (physical and mental), so ensuring quality in these areas sets the stage for resiliency.

Channel your emotions into creative outlets. Be it through art, writing, music, or other creative outlets; these activities can help us pour out our inner chaos and let that emotion grow to become a part of genuine expression.

We are not kind or compassionate towards ourselves. We recognize that we all have internal battles, and there is no shame in needing help. If you do not speak like that to a friend who is suffering, then you should not be speaking like that to yourself.

Developing healthy coping skills to deal with stress and feelings of overwhelm may involve deep breathing, writing in a journal, or engaging in any pleasurable and relaxing activity.

Realize and embrace that we are human and imperfection is part of our nature. Please remember that we build our souls through challenges, persistence, and sometimes hardship, not by renouncing every failure.

MASTERING FRUSTRATION

Do not regard setbacks as failures; see them as opportunities for learning and development. Reflect on what went awry, take notes of lessons learned, and then use that to shape your next steps.

Small wins count, so do not forget to celebrate. Accept the long journey you embarked on yourself to put into action a more constructive and more resilient mindset than the one that led you astray.

Ultimately, struggling with inner demons is an individual struggle that cannot be solved through any method without first looking within yourself and being willing to grow. But with these tools running through one lateral, one might be able to face those internal battles and arrive at a destination for better mental health.

MASTERING FRUSTRATION

Chapter 8

Releasing Inner Frustration

Has it ever felt like there's a storm brewing inside you? Resentment and inner turmoil are storms in their own right—a cyclone of emotions, thoughts, and pent-up energy. This type of storm is as destructive as it is powerful, leaving a lasting impact on both your emotional and physical well-being.

If we are going to gain some control over this frustration, we must acknowledge it exists within us. It is something to understand, not to fear. It's like an old friend who has loitered in your life for too long and is making everything worse. You'd talk to them before kicking them out, right?

The Power of Release
Releasing internal frustration feels like releasing a pressure valve. Sharing that energy helps not just your mood but also your whole body. The tension subsides, headaches disappear, and a calm settles in. So, how do you initiate this release process?

The Power of Awareness

The first circle of mastering anything is awareness.

To overcome frustration, you must identify it when it strikes, just like knowing your enemy on the battlefield. Until you can locate it, you will not know how to deal with it.

Think for a moment about yourself. Have you been angry lately? Perhaps it was with technology, at work, or in your marriage. To overcome things that cause frustration, you need to understand at what level and where they invade your life.

Identify the source of your internal discontentment. Is it unfinished business, unmet needs, or feeling out of control? Mark the boundaries around a source. Setting up boundaries in your life has strong potential. It creates a boundary to care for your emotional health so you don't get frustrated internally.

Here's some healthy, constructive release for all of your ire: Practice mindfulness through journaling, talking to a friend, or exercising. Stay in the present moment without judging yourself for feeling what you feel. With mindfulness, you can take a step back and respond more clearly and with self-compassion to frustration.

Letting Go and Moving Forward

MASTERING FRUSTRATION

Getting inner frustration out is not a one-time thing; you do it for life. Finding time to exercise your mental health is the same as being fit and healthy. With time, this becomes easier as you unbottle inner frustration and let the storms within you slowly settle.

This is not about eliminating frustration from your life (that would be impossible). It's possibly the most challenging thing to realize, but instead of getting rid of it, it's about learning how to cope and ensuring it doesn't become a destructive beast. It's like taming a wild river; it may trickle, but it's under control.

MASTERING FRUSTRATION

Chapter 9

Navigating Workplace Difficulties

Workplace frustration comes from the everyday demands of our jobs mixed with not-very-calming pet peeves. Free your mind from following them. It might be long hours of working, unrealistic expectations set by your bosses/management, or lousy communication among the team. Frustrations of this kind can significantly affect your career.

Consider getting a job in a company where projects are thrashed at the last moment and documentation on what needs to be implemented is unclear. This can quickly become frustrating, which is bad for your job satisfaction and health.

Sarah is a driven and hardworking project manager in charge of a high-stakes cross-functional team assembling to wrap up an essential piece of work by the deadline. Sarah demands excellence from herself and the team to meet deadlines and achieve high performance throughout this project.

However, as the project develops, Sarah sees there is a misalignment of expectations. A few of my teammates, keen on work-life balance, prefer to follow the standard working hours and are reluctant to do what is needed. In contrast, Sarah is more passionate about getting the project done and demands much more dedication from her employees, even asking them to stay longer if needed.

This conflict of expectations comes to a head at a crucial stage in the project. When Sarah, under the time pressure of an impending deadline, expects a collaborative push and her colleagues adhere unwaveringly to their working hours, it creates a bottleneck in the workflow. As a result, the team feels pressured by Sarah's implicit expectations, leaving them demoralized and stressed.

Embodying the extreme version of the "the customer is always right" mentality, Sarah believes in exceeding expectations. In contrast, her team believes in a work-life balance. This imbalance between Sarah and the team leads to frustration, as Sarah feels unsupported while team members think they're under pressure to meet unreasonable requirements.

The above example highlights the need to communicate openly and set expectations in workplace relationships. It also shows the importance of a fine line between what an individual expects and needs to give in collaboration. Understanding and addressing these interpersonal dynamics can help ensure both parties a more productive, pleasurable professional experience.

Work can be rewarding but often a breeding ground for frustration. Office political pressures, short deadlines, insensitive fellow team members, and unrelenting bosses can easily lead to this emotion. Knowing how to deal with professional frustration effectively is a good skill.

The cost of workplace frustration can be steep if you leave to run amok. It may simmer down your enjoyment at work, rise to stress, disrupt relations with colleges, and possibly inflict blame on your growth. The first step to tackle this is realizing the cost of unmanaged workplace frustration.

Job-Related Stressors: The Challenge
Job stress is an enormous and universal concern of today for everyone in the professional field, irrespective of their profession or industry. It is no secret that workplace stressors significantly impact employees' mental and physical health. Identifying and addressing these stressors is necessary for developing a healthier, more productive work environment. Now, essential facets relating to the challenge of job stressors:

A) Type of Stressors Related to Job:
Heavy workloads, tight deadlines, and high expectations create pressure. Conflicts with colleagues, supervisors, or subordinates can heighten stress, while job insecurity adds further strain. A lack of control over work and decisions is also stressful. Inability to balance work and personal life contributes to chronic stress, as does insufficient support, such as limited counseling or stress management resources.

WORK-RELATED FRUSTRATION
Relates to job-related stress that may lead to mental health issues (e.g., anxiety, depression). This stress and the expectation take a toll on a person's psychological state. When someone is exposed to job-related stressors for an extended period, they may develop physical health problems, which could include cardiovascular disease or musculoskeletal disorders and compromise the pulmonary system.

Ongoing stress can diminish job satisfaction, which can reduce motivation and involvement. This can then, in turn, affect overall job performance and organizational success.

Chronic stress can reduce cognitive function, decision-making, and problem-solving, which can harm productivity and the quality of work.

Job stressors are not confined to impacting individual employees; they also impact the workplace as a whole, such as absenteeism and turnover, and there may be an overall down moment.

Cultural and Leadership-Related Pressure Points:
The organization's culture and leadership styles organically create the workplace. A culture of openness and communication and the right kind of leadership can alleviate stress and promote employee wellness. Organizations can reduce the ill effects caused by work stress by ensuring that there are programs for developing stress management.

Significance of Stress Management Programs:
A growing number of organizations recognize that the current state of job-related stressors calls for a broad-ranging approach to reducing and managing them. This is based on an increasing understanding of how workplace stress affects employees' well-being, productivity, and job happiness. Several organizations will incorporate stress management programs, wellness initiatives, and mental health resources to pursue a healthier workplace.

Advantages of Stress Management Programs:

Organizations that have implemented stress management programs with the goal of mitigating workplace stress by giving their employees appropriate tools to cope are starting to see a return on investment (ROI) through employee productivity. These programs may consist of special workshops, training classes, and resources that can help you become stronger with stress and improve your time management skills and emotional intelligence.

Wellness initiatives that address the whole person are vital to organizational strategies to improve employee well-being. These efforts span the physical, mental, and emotional domains, encompassing fitness programming, nutrition support, mindfulness practices, and work-life balance initiatives.

Organizations develop dedicated support services to focus on mental health because they know its importance. This could mean providing counseling services, employee assistance programs (EAPs), or collaborating with mental health professionals to provide discreet and accessible support pathways.

Flexible Work Arrangement: Another proactive step to decrease stress is providing a flexible work arrangement, such as allowing employees to work from home when they feel like it or giving them the option of having a flexible working schedule. Autonomy gives employees the freedom to work in a way that suits their personal needs, which creates control and balance.

Establish Transparent Communication Channels: This step is crucial in curbing job stressors. Encouraging a culture of voicing concerns, seeking help when needed, and being able to provide feedback about the workplace are things organizations are urging.

Workload management training should assist employees in establishing priorities, defining achievable purposes, and managing their precious time. This proactive strategy helps to avoid stress and enables employees to adjust better to job demands.

Invest more in leadership training to ensure managers know how to support the well-being of their employees. Workplace culture, recognizing when team members are under pressure, and adopting a leadership style that focuses on the team's health should all form part of a behavioral change program.

Promote favorable work conditions to support employee health and wellness. Organizations can redesign workspaces and improve workplace cultures to foster a more supportive and inclusive environment. That includes policies that do not promote overwork, fostering a sense of community and belonging, and appreciating that diversity, equity, inclusion, and accessibility contribute to well-being.

Promote physical health indicators. Employers can provide Regular health check-ups or wellness screenings to monitor their employees' physical well-being. This can mitigate unaffordable stress from unmanaged health issues and proactively reduce employee health risks.

Encouraging social connections is vital for worker wellness. Organizations that recognize how these connections buffer stress can foster a positive workplace culture through team-building activities, social events, and mentorship programs.

This will help organizations have an environment that can identify and mitigate stress factors at work while also providing mechanisms for employees to reach out when needed to maintain their well-being proactively. The holistic domain showcases that the safety of the employees involves more than just individual awareness but also a collective responsibility between the organization and its workers.

Coping Mechanisms of the Individual/Worker:

MASTERING FRUSTRATION

Establishing personal coping mechanisms, such as time management, realistic goal setting, social support, and engaging in relaxation and wellness activities, can benefit employees.

Understanding and managing your emotions and those of your fellow workers is also essential. When you practice emotional intelligence, working through workplace frustrations becomes more accessible, leading to healthier work relationships.

Effective communication can often remedy workplace frustrations. However, knowing how to say what you want and feel and listening with an open mind can lead to explosive situations.

When we feel pressured and time-scarce, frustration often ensues. Understanding how to effectively manage your time will alleviate some frustration in the workplace and can help you become more productive.

At the workplace, conflict is one of those things people get most pissed off about. Conflict resolution skills can help you handle disputes professionally rather than have constant frustration.

Setting boundaries is an essential part of dealing with workplace frustration. Boundaries are crucial for clarifying what you will and won't accept in your work life. They defend your emotional well-being and keep you in the work-life balance.

Setting boundaries around work is essential for maintaining overall well-being and a healthy work-life balance. This can be achieved by establishing specific work hours to separate personal time, creating a designated workspace to mentally distinguish between work and home, and delegating tasks when possible. By allowing others to take ownership of certain responsibilities, you can focus on tasks that align with your strengths and priorities, ultimately enhancing productivity and reducing stress.

Set clear boundaries around your availability to manage expectations and avoid taking on tasks outside your role. Defining responsibilities helps prevent overburdening yourself and reduces the risk of burnout. Remember, it's okay to say no to new responsibilities and commitments—taking on too much can negatively impact both your well-being and the quality of your work.

Set a limit for phone calls, emails, and messages when working from home. It prevents the urge to be connected constantly and allows personal time to remain respected. Establish designated periods when you will deal with emails and notifications. Do not disturb yourself by checking your email now and then.

MASTERING FRUSTRATION

Take some time off from work each day to reset and recharge. This boundary keeps work from becoming an endless slog. Use the leave plan and take annual leave as necessary. Boundaries around holidays and time off serve as barriers, protecting us from the stressors of work and allowing for much-needed recovery and relaxation.

If you feel overtime hours are part of the stressor, set boundaries. Overtime is unavoidable sometimes, but working overtime regularly can burn someone out and decrease productivity. Understand that your work is much more important than the amount of work that needs to be done. Cancel marching orders because whenever we are multitasking, our focus on the work decreases, and stress increases. Work on one task at a time and prioritize it to be more efficient.

Set aside some time for your projects or activities outside of work. That might involve doing something else, such as a hobby, spending time with family, or working on self-improvement.

Put yourself first; self-care is not up for negotiation. Make boundaries so that regular exercise, enough sleep, and the rest of the self-care happen. For working from home, create boundaries for working consistently. Set a beginning and ending time to prevent work-life balance boundaries from starting to overlap. Have tech detox phases, especially outside of working hours. Minimise screen time and do not use any work-related technology to help you feel more relaxed.

Check out productivity tools and apps that help to manage tasks, deadlines, and schedules. Calendar, to-do lists, and project management tools—each app can make us more organized and help us work better. Group related tasks together and complete them during specific time blocks on a single day. Task batching reduces cognitive switching and enables more focused and efficient work. Establish rituals that mark the transition from work to after-work time. This could be taking a short walk, doing some afternoon meditation, or doing anything that allows you to change gears mentally. Be firm about your boundaries and respond every time they are crossed.

They are imperative for a good work-life balance, to prevent burnout, and to improve overall health.

A huge part of mastering this tricky emotion is navigating workplace frustration. Armed with the right tools and a somewhat nuanced grasp of how frustration shows up in your work life, you are one step closer to conquering that familiar feeling and creating greater peace and pleasure around the workplace.

All in all, job stressors must be solved organically through teamwork from institutes and individuals. Reducing these stressors requires dedication to building a healthy workplace culture, creating proper stress management programs and regimes, and opening lines of communication on ways we can better promote employees' mental and physical health.

Chapter 10

Navigating Frustration in Education

Academic frustration is the emotional and psychological response to challenges, difficulties, or setbacks in an educational context. It can be experienced on multiple levels of the educational pipeline, from primary years to secondary to post-secondary and beyond. Academic frustration is a collection of scenarios that prevent learning or stop progression. It will usually leave one feeling frustrated with academic studies.

Jamie is a high-achieving student pursuing an engineering degree. He works part-time and manages many extracurricular commitments. His enthusiasm for his studies fuels his desire to excel, and he is eager to get hands-on experience while being an active campus community member.

Nevertheless, this complexity of duties serves as an interpersonal relationship irritant. Academic expectations require substantial time for classes, assignments, and tests. At the same time, part-time work is a necessity—not just a filler—in the ever-more expensive world, adding another layer of time and energy cost to it. In addition, Jamie participates in other student clubs, and that is how she will impact life outside of the classroom.

When academic deadlines are on the same day as work shifts and club meetings, it becomes more evident that these expectations clash. Jamie's drive to succeed in every aspect of life results in a precarious balancing act, where the fear of failure looms large from all sides. This juggling of different expectations weighs on Jamie, hurting his happiness and health.

The frustration is about juggling academic, professional, and extracurricular performance expectations. This quest for mastery at every competing front induces strain and the perpetual battle of time. Good prioritization and time management techniques are vital, as are regular open dialogues with professors, employers, or club members, to keep student life from getting too complicated.

Through her experience, she learned that expectations must be realistic, that it is okay to ask for help, and that balancing school, work, and other activities must be attempted. Comprehending that time and energy are finite can create a more sustainable and rewarding experience in student life.

Some Common Academic Frustration Triggers:
Academic frustration often occurs when students struggle to understand complex concepts or learn a subject. Struggling to comprehend, note down, and remember material can breed a feeling of embarrassment and despair when grades are high but expectations are even higher.

Academic frustration can arise mainly due to the requirement of ongoing assignments, projects, and exams. Unrealistic time limits, vague instructions, or the pressure of being constantly scrutinized can create anxiety, which harms learning and undermines confidence.

Without access to all the educational resources or support from teachers or peers, limited infrastructure will cause that frustration to grow academically. Lack of access to tools or proper direction fosters a challenging learning environment, making academic success nearly impossible.

Personal issues, school conflicts, or outside distractions can lead to academic frustration. Health, family problems, or environmental disruptions may affect a person's focus and participation in scholarly pursuits.

Failing exams, struggling academically, or not meeting societal or personal expectations can lead to significant frustration. That fear could be internal pressure or external forcing, resulting in a red alert of the emotional system and preventing advancement in academia.

Repeated academic failure may result in a lack of motivation and engagement with subsequent educational tasks. This may cause people to feel disheartened, so they exert less effort and focus on their studies.

Adverse effects on mental health:
Poor academic performance can lead to stress, anxiety, and feelings of inadequacy, which can take a toll on mental health. The continuous fight against academic difficulties can cause feelings of stress and high levels of emotional burnout.

Repeated academic failure can undermine self-esteem and confidence. Doubts, self-criticism, and lack of faith in academic ability gradually decrease students' confidence.

It can cause learning to backtrack and academic performance to fall. Emotional baggage might suppress the sense of joy in learning, causing students to miss their full educational potential.

MASTERING FRUSTRATION

Dealing with academic frustration requires a holistic, preventative mindset approach since many aspects of the student life cycle influence a student's academic experience. Academic frustration stems from various circumstances and scenarios that make an individual experience varying degrees of emotional and intellectual pressure to succeed in their educational pursuit. However, there are methods to maneuver around those challenges, such as asking your teacher or mentor for guidance, productive study habits, or simply having a good attitude toward challenges you may face.

Good study habits are an essential remedy for academic trouble. These include devising a realistic revision timetable, splitting complex topics into more manageable sets, and adopting forms of active recall. A healthy study environment provides a more distraction-free and focused study session.

Setting realistic and attainable academic expectations makes regulating a student more accessible and minimizes frustration. Splitting long-term goals into smaller, achievable milestones fosters a feeling of accomplishment and motivation, which helps them maintain a positive attitude toward their studies.

Balancing all the academic burdens requires effective time management techniques. Prioritizing your tasks, scheduling time to study, and establishing deadlines for coursework allow students to have a much less hectic school experience. List down and prioritize tasks by combining urgency and importance.

Starting with high-priority items doesn't just let you focus on essential duties. It also reduces stress and saves us from an end crisis. Find out potential distractions and minimize them. Silence unnecessary alerts, set up a particular work area, and let people know not to disturb you so you can work without interruptions. Understand the value of saying no when needed. The downside of staying busy is burnout and less quality work. Put the brakes on taking on new responsibilities and other obligations.

A growth mindset means seeing challenges not as barriers to success but as opportunities for learning and growth. A positive attitude towards failure cultivates resilience, flexibility, and a desire to persist through other academic challenges.

Consistent self-analysis helps students evaluate their learning methods, highlight factors that need change, and identify their strengths. Knowing your learning styles brings you closer to understanding how you operate academically and best adapt your study habits.

MASTERING FRUSTRATION

Many institutions provide free services such as tutoring or study groups, which are great supplementary outlets for support. Working with your classmates and having extra resources to fill in knowledge gaps can give more clarity on the topic, leading to less confusion.

Balancing academics and non-academic life is crucial to maintaining overall well-being. Including breaks, recreational activities, and free time in the daily regimen prevents burnout and fosters a balanced response to academic endeavors.

Using Edtech can improve the whole learning process. Online resources, educational applications, and digital tools designed for specific subjects can further assist traditional learning techniques and offer additional assistance and diverse learning opportunities.

Focusing on small academic achievements and celebrating those strengthens a positive academic mindset. Seeing progress, grasping complex topics, and completing exercises provide students with a sense of accomplishment, fueling their motivation.

If you're feeling particularly frustrated academically, one of the most important things you can do is to reach out to a teacher or mentor. You are clarifying complex concepts, taking advantage of problems during or after class, and attending office hours to address academic issues. Creating channels for open communication gives students a space to feel supported.

These solutions can also be used in conjunction with one another to develop a preventive plan against academic-related distress among students. Such a holistic perspective reminds us that academic success is not only about cramming for term exams but also about creating good learning habits, reaching out for help, and maintaining a growth mindset toward challenges.

Chapter 11

Navigating Frustration in Relationships

There is no denying that relationships are complicated. They involve emotions, communication, expectations, and personal histories. Combine those styles and throw in individual personalities, needs, and experience complexities. You have a relationship bubble that is both intoxicating (in an upside-down, right-side-up kind of way) and intriguing.

Consider your relationships with friends, partners, family, and colleagues. Each has its conditional requirements and expectations, which can be everchanging and require constant work and awareness to remain in effect.

For instance, a romantic relationship may be balanced between personal values and shared dreams, while family dynamics are filled with love and obligation but often also competition. They can be a wild ride of support and laughter, but with time, they also need both sides to keep the wheels from falling off.

Relationships are often a blend of joy and happiness, as well as crises and frustrations. The complexities of maintaining healthy human relationships embody the enduring fractions that can impact everyone. Even these crises and frustrations are rooted in the differences between human beings because each person is unique, and their experiences may vary, leading to different expectations. In addition, external pressure affects their relations.

Unrealistic expectations, miscommunication, or a clash of individual needs and wants can lead to relationship frustrations. Frustration can grow when expectations are not met. However, discrepancies and breakdowns in communication can result in emotional tension, confusion, or discontent. There are many relationship crises and frustrations; addressing them with understanding and communication remains the key. Common Relationship Problems With Examples

Lack of clarity in communication or misunderstandings can entail frustration for partners. As a result, they might feel like nobody is listening or no one understands them. An equally annoying situation in the complex web of relationships is that communication breakdown or struggle could stem from one partner choosing to keep certain information private. This behavior can become very infuriating—especially when it involves something important that impacts both partners but is kept quiet. The cracks in openness are evident when the other partner learns of the secret and starts to follow that technique of holding whatever is personal.

Unfortunately, this choice ends up damaging the relationship.

Partner A may decide not to tell her partner about a huge financial decision that ultimately affects them to respect the lines between each other's personal lives. Partner A feels this is the only way to avoid what they see as an unnecessary invasion of their lives. However, the consequences are severe when Partner B discovers this information was never disclosed. Partner B retaliates by leading the same private life in response to feeling hurt and left out.

It starts a new cycle in which both partners intentionally or unintentionally work together to dissolve the presence of healthy expression further. Issues that were once openly discussed are now kept private for the sake of privacy, often without realizing that this emotional distance affects both partners. Initially, it seemed like a way to preserve personal space, but over time, it became a barrier that prevents the exchange of essential information crucial for a healthy relationship. This communication gap leads to frustration, misinterpretations, and a feeling of general separation. What began as private so we could have individual autonomy has become a rolling ball chipping away at the shared atmosphere of trust and transparency.

Partners should understand that both confidentiality and openness are a delicate balance. Boundaries can be set to respect privacy but not at the expense of excluding critical matters from the partnership. Generous conversation, enormous trust, and the commitment to cooperation in decision-making between couples will ultimately go the distance to ensure a healthy and happy relationship.

Issues like mistrust in a relationship are caused mainly by lying or betrayal. The aftereffects of these experiences can range from being predisposed to suspect something sinister is afoot to an ongoing, pervasive sense of insecurity or even needing to muster a dearth of justifiable effort to genuinely process and internally accept a partner's words or behaviors as accurately as possible.

A situation would be if a partner realizes their lover has been hiding bits from their life, eventually making the partner feel betrayed. When a partner engages in infidelity, financial secrecy, or other deceptive behaviors, trust becomes broken over time, and they become the trigger for the development process of some misunderstanding regarding trust.

It takes a long time for the injured partner to heal after discovering that their partner's love isn't true. The hurt partner is skeptical toward every action and statement and attempts to bridge the gap made by the partner who committed betrayal.

The injured partner may never quite feel good enough or live in the trepidation of being betrayed again, and insecurity can poison every aspect of the next relationship. However, this emotional vulnerability can cast a shadow on the bond between two parties and affect how security and stability are perceived in the sexual relationship.

Trust issues are characterized by difficulty believing what the partner says or does. Despite the partner's genuine attempts or intentions to convince them otherwise, the injured party may not always be able to embrace that sincerity because they are still marked with broken trust.

Rebuilding trust takes work from both partners. The rebuilding of trust takes straightforward correspondence, an assurance of truthfulness, and the ability to admit and amend previous wrongdoings. For those still struggling with trust issues, professional help is often crucial in working through this complex subject and feeling safer within the relationship again.

The absence of emotional or physical intimacy in a relationship can leave couples feeling out of sync, neglected, unappreciated, and disconnected, ultimately impacting their overall satisfaction.

Picture this: a once inseparable sexual and emotional bond between partners seems to be progressively fading. With emotional and physical intimacy reviewed, one or both partners may experience an emptiness that results in frustration and resentment of unfulfilled needs.

That lack of emotional intimacy may look like less time spent together, limited conversation, or a disconnect in understanding and connection. The absence of physical touch may also mean less affectionate touch, intimacy in shared activities, or a reduction in sexual intimacy.

When partners pick up from the relationship that there isn't much focus on their emotional or physical well-being, this feeling of neglect may get into overdrive. This may lead to feeling unappreciated or undervalued, which could be a breeding ground for even more frustration and discontent.

Because intimacy issues impact the relationship as a whole, they can diminish both partners' satisfaction and fulfillment with each other. Addressing these worries requires two partners whose hearts are open, who want to understand each other's needs, and who are willing to reinvigorate the emotional or physical attraction that brought them together in the first place.

Finding ways to reignite intimacy, whether having deeper conversations, making time for each other, or sharing physical affection, may usher in the connection you seek. Professional help, like couples counseling, may also help address intimacy issues and work together to feel satisfied in this part of your relationship again.

MASTERING FRUSTRATION

Conflicting financial priorities, spending habits, or differences in attitudes about money can lead to significant stress that breeds frustration. When couples start to argue about some money-related things, this naturally leads to a financial strain on that relationship.

For example, one partner could focus on long-term financial health and discuss savings. On the other hand, one partner likes to have a more relaxing and immediate present life and is ready to pay for it. The conflicting views of financial priorities create an irritable and bothersome static between partners, each scrambling to understand the other's vision of how finances should be managed or distributed.

Financial strain is more than the ability to make ends meet; it touches on what each partner values and expects from one another regarding money. Differences in spending habits or lack of alignment with financial goals can cause a breakdown of communication and understanding, leading to even more stress on the relationship.

Financial stress can turn from a banging headache to fights, resentment, and feeling financially unsupported. Cash is another significant source of stress for couples, and they get frustrated when they think their partner doesn't understand where they are coming from.

Discussing financial strain involves talking about one's outlook, priorities, and goals. This conversation can be approached openly and intentionally, fostering understanding and clarity on how to navigate financial challenges.

Listening to professional financial counseling or couples therapy about how best to navigate financial strain can also help partners build a foundation of money harmony that will be part of a healthy relationship.

However, conflicts can occur where one partner has more power and control than the other. These could revolve around our decisions, tasks, jobs, or standing up for what we want. A dispute may arise as an abuse of authority or influence in a given context. That imbalance shows up in decision-making, work distribution, or how individual needs are expressed and could lead to friction and disagreement.

Picture this: One partner makes decisions that often make the other feel inferior and unable to make choices. This creates a power struggle, sparking conflict between them. The imbalance may extend to the division of labor, with one partner shouldering an unfair share, deepening the power disparity.

Power play may also become apparent when expressing or prioritizing personal needs. A partner who constantly places their needs or wants over the other is guaranteed to cause frustration and resentment, breeding an imbalance in the relationship.

Such discord could undermine the respect and collaborative spirit on which a warm, reciprocal relationship grows. One partner may feel like they have zero influence, making them feel unheard or undervalued; the other may not fully understand how their behavior affects their less powerful partner.

To combat the power struggles, we must ensure that both partners can express their needs, wants, and fears openly and honestly. Establishing some balance (decisions and responsibility) will help achieve a healthy dynamic. Finding a way to rewrite the power dynamics of any relationship, be it professional or personal, is critical since we all know that at least one person has more of a leg up. This makes seeking out mutual respect, autonomy, and compromise vital.

Couples can also consider seeing a relationship counselor or therapist to help them work through the power struggles. By working towards building a collaborative and cooperative style, the partners will do it in a much healthier way, and at least both partners will feel seen, validated, and empowered.

A clash of values, expectations, or even interference from either side of the extended family can lead to tensions. Interference from extended family members can be annoying when they hijack a relationship because people simply do not want to let go. Finding a fine line regarding your relationship with the in-laws and setting boundaries is essential to keeping a healthy relationship.

Imagine partners coming to their relationship from different cultural or familial backgrounds and thus holding unique values, expectations, etc. These differences can often cause misunderstandings and disputes, as well as frustrate both parties while they have to adjust their past to the dynamics of their joined life.

The pressure of extended family can make these problems even worse. The experience of unsolicited but well-meaning advice, conflicting expectations, or an absence of privacy might also be a source of friction in the relationship. What drives the frustration is the natural instinct to fight for independence and create one's own little world despite these external forces.

Managing in-law relationships requires open communication and a commitment to understanding and honoring each other's family backgrounds. Setting firm boundaries becomes crucial. That might mean limiting how involved anyone gets in your personal lives, collaboratively deciding on boundaries when it comes to family events, and creating an independent unit that is respectful of family.

Couples struggling with family and in-law politics may consider couples counseling or family therapy for guidance. Therapy can aid by providing tools for communication, boundary setting, and navigating complicated relationships.

By discussing these dynamics and allowing space for both partners to express their needs openly, the couple can work towards creating a new environment in which one family is not at odds with another but nurtured by it while building their family unit.

Stressors can come into play during significant life changes, like losing a job, moving to another city or country, or starting a family. It can get frustrating if the new roles and responsibilities are improperly handled. Failure to adjust accordingly could make adapting to new roles and responsibilities during these times an unbearable frustration.

Imagine a situation in which a couple that lives a comfortable life and has both jobs faces an unexpected turn of events, such as their job getting terminated. This can be particularly challenging as the emotional impact of this transition takes a toll. Still, increasingly, both partners feel the financial strain, and many couples have seen that pressure affect tensions in their relationship, constantly working to meet expectations and adapt to newfound uncertainties. This frustration comes from renegotiating roles and managing expectations while dealing with the transition's emotional and mental cost.

Likewise, while the beginning of a family unit can be incredibly energizing, it can also come with pressure from things like reframing your needs around your schedule, lack of sleep, and changes to the allotment of obligations. Becoming a parent is the most significant adjustment most couples will ever have to deal with, and this blog points out that even though both spouses love their new child very much, it can put significant strain on the relationship.

Moving for a job or family reasons presents a whole new dilemma. First, there's the challenge of communicating frustrations about adjusting to a new climate, making new friends, and navigating the transition together. This combination of stresses can easily lead to frustrations directed at each other.

Transitioning through life changes is best done together. During these transitions, partners should express their expectations, fears, and needs. Having friends, family members, or professional counseling can go a long way toward supporting the stress of life changes.

After all, everyone goes through transitions—it helps to remember that the other person might also be experiencing challenges. When couples navigate the ins and outs of change, potential frustration can become a gift that builds resilience and strengthens their connection.

Frustration can arise when one partner forms emotional connections outside the relationship that cross a comfort threshold. Sharing emotions or ideas with someone else can create tension, undermining the relationship's stability.

Now imagine one partner sharing intimate things with a coworker or friend, creating an emotional bond that exceeds the boundaries of their relationship. However, this compromises emotional exclusivity, which results in the other partner developing feelings of frustration, betrayal, and self-doubt.

This is frustrating because the trust and emotional connection in the relationship have been eroded. This passing of emotional energy that was once shared solely between partners also provides opportunities for resentment, as the partner who is not in the triangle may begin to feel neglected or shut out emotionally. Being replaced or not being the main confidant can amplify the emotional toll of this type of infidelity.

Emotional infidelity requires effort—through open and honest communication. Rebuilding trust involves acknowledging the impact of the breach and intentionally restoring the emotional connection in the relationship.

It can help couples consult a relationship counselor or therapist to help guide them through the complex issues involved in emotional infidelity. Some tools they may provide are professional ways to communicate, build trust again, and create a safe space for an emotionally healthy relationship.

When it comes to how serious the relationship is, what they do a few weekends out of the year, or how much longer this will last—frustration often arises when one partner feels their expectations are not being met by the other. Sometimes, partners have different perspectives on commitment, plans, or the direction of their relationship, which creates mismatched expectations. As a result, when both partners are on other pages of the book, it leads to irritation more than anything else.

Imagine a situation where one partner sees them as something more than that and envisions a long-term commitment or marriage, while the other is looking for more of a casual arrangement. Then, the frustration of reconciling expectations around how serious one partner thinks it is versus what another may want in terms of direction will stir and clash between them both.

If you have certain timed expectations like having a baby or moving in together, another source of frustration could arise if you're not both on top of the same life goals sooner rather than later. Realizing

MASTERING FRUSTRATION

that partners do not meet the exact expectations can be frustrating and sometimes devastating.

But when expecting different things, the best way forward is communication—that means being transparent and listening. Early on in the relationship, couples should talk about their individual expectations, values, and long-term goals. By combating potential differences beforehand, you can start making decisions together and agree on a middle ground.

Finding your way through these differences might require compromise, assessing individual priorities, and an ever-present dedication to communication and understanding. If, despite your efforts, things still seem disconnected, a relationship counselor or therapist might also be needed to assist with the confusion of mismatched expectations and ways that bring both partners into a connection that best reflects their shared image.

A lack of recognition, respect, or appreciation can be frustrating. Partners may want acknowledgment and affirmation for what they have brought to the relationship. No appreciation in a relationship can create frustration. This is born from a desire for validation and positive acknowledgment of how each partner contributes to the couple.

Consider a situation where one couple member puts effort into the relationship—whether to arrange daily activities like taking out the trash, providing emotional support, or doing chores. If these attempts are not recognized, the participating partner may feel frustrated as they will think their efforts are overlooked.

The need to feel appreciated stems from the basic human need for belonging and connectedness. Partners may even need recognition for the big things you do outside the spotlight to care for your home, life, and relationship.

Dealing with appreciated things means openly communicating their importance in the relationship. Couples are then coached to articulate their recognition needs and acknowledge each other. A culture of appreciation—showing appreciation for small wins and significant victories reinforces that each partner's contributions are appreciated.

If neither partner feels appreciated, or one does not feel seen at all, then periodic reminders of this nature lead to resentment — and this is the wrong type of communication; communication continues to be crucial, but so does releasing what is needed. It can help couples engage in activities that show appreciation, such as saying and writing thanks or doing something thoughtful to acknowledge what you have done. The above mindful practice of appreciation helps create a better and healthier relationship.

MASTERING FRUSTRATION

Personality trait incompatibilities, communication style differences, or approaches to conflict resolution can result in ongoing frustration with the marriage unless those issues are addressed. Personality clashes can occur between people with incompatible personality traits, differing communication styles, or completely different approaches to conflict resolution. These divergences can cause continuous frustration between partners if not dealt with.

Example: One partner is an extrovert who loves to socialize and enjoys a good party or going out on weekends, while the other partner is an introvert who prefers solitude, quietness, and planned activities. It can create frustration when both partners must deal with the fact that different styles require compromises.

Personality clashes are also partly a result of different communication styles. For example, we may have one partner who is confident and direct in their communication style and another who is quieter or passive. Such differences in communication styles can lead to misunderstandings and empathy when there is no fault on either side, and both partners struggle with compelling and harmonious interaction.

Different conflict resolution styles may cause continued frustration, with one partner preferring to talk things through while the other shying away from confrontation altogether. Failure to resolve such discrepancies may result in unresolved problems and alienation within any relationship.

Solutions to personality clashes include communication and understanding of the other unit. This focuses on nurturing awareness of differences and expressing appreciation for what is unique in the other person to foster feelings of connection rather than conflict over why one partner prefers certain things that are different from those with which the other partner identifies. Finding communication strategies that work for both partners and are in both of your styles can improve understanding and lessen frustration.

Couples who want to take advantage of their differences more may benefit from activities that champion those distinctions and offer room for compromise. Consulting a couple of therapists or helpful resources can provide perspective and competencies for overcoming personality differences in a way that leads to a well-integrated partnership.

It may be due to insecurity or a sense of jealousy with no foundation, which could stem from past experiences or emotional vulnerabilities. Unwelcome lust or extreme indecisiveness in a romance can happen from otherwise baseless emotions of envy and deficiency of trust in either spouse—frequently based on early bruising, sad experiences, and psychological frailty.

Suppose your partner may become highly suspicious or possessive without evidence due to past betrayals or personal insecurities. This uneasiness will trigger a problem with the relationship as the other partner directs you to learn how to earn and build trust.

Insecurity can manifest in various behaviors, such as questioning one's value, fearing abandonment, and feeling threatened by perceived external factors that may jeopardize the relationship.

Communicating openly and honestly about where jealousy and insecurity stem from goes a long way. Partners can reveal their vulnerabilities, admit they need reassurance, and collaborate to build trust and security.

Overcoming the underlying triggers driving jealousy and insecurity takes time, trust, and effort. Engage in activities that help to create trust and provide outlets for emotional support. It might also be helpful to discuss it with a relationship counselor or therapist to understand the complexities of these emotions better and learn ways to create a more healthy, secure bond.

Unresolved issues can persist, leading to future conflicts that harm the relationship's health. For a relationship to thrive, all aspects must function smoothly. Lingering issues should be resolved, or they'll affect even the smallest matters and fuel frustration.

Now imagine this couple going through a severe conflict, misunderstanding, or argument, and rather than tackling the root issues, they choose to bypass or bury the conflict. Those unresolved issues can simmer for years, generating frustration as the unanswered tensions shape the relationship.

This frustration can show itself in different forms, such as a gap in communication, feeling not emotionally close, or an ever-increasing rate of resentment. To go in circles, come back again and again to the same issue, unable to overcome and move forward with a solution.

Navigating lingering disagreements takes initiative and a willingness to listen. Therapist Colleen O'Grady recommends that couples set up an environment where they can talk freely. Both parties should listen to each other and meet in the middle, or at least on common ground.

A relationship counselor or therapist can offer helpful tools if you need to resolve conflicts. Therapy enables couples to dig deeper into their emotions and learn why these arguments are surfacing, discover positive communication tools, create solutions that foster the health of their relationship, or make other changes necessary for stability.

MASTERING FRUSTRATION

Being overpowered by your partner's excessive work commitments, social obligations, or other priorities can leave you feeling frustrated and emotionally distant. If you work long hours every day and your partner is at home (alone), this imbalance in time and attention will eventually create an emotional deficit. Without this balance, one can become frustrated and emotionally distanced.

Consider a situation in which your partner is constantly busy with work, social events, or other pursuits that leave no time or attention for your relationship. One partner feels shut out, and the lack of quality time spent together nurtures resentment if they feel they are being neglected emotionally.

This disparity can result in loneliness, lack of emotional fulfillment, or even possible separation, leading to resentment from an imbalance in time and attention. When one partner invests way more time and attention into the relationship than the other, it creates a complex and problematic situation for the partner who receives adverse effects.

Communicating the need for time and attention is essential to ensure both partners understand that, despite life's busyness, prioritizing the relationship remains important. Couples should talk about what they need to feel connected and, when possible, address obstacles or limitations standing in the way.

Maybe you need to limit work or social obligations, dedicate time to something you can do together, or try getting back in touch emotionally. In other words, it is up to both partners to establish an atmosphere in their relationship where each feels important, listened to, and emotionally bonded.

Couples with imbalanced time and attention could benefit from relationship counseling or therapy. By seeking professional assistance with the above questions and issues, partners can be guided to effectively cope with such imbalance for a healthier and more satisfying union.

Frustration arises when people feel that a relationship has sacrificed their freedom or independence. When they perceive their choices as limited, it can lead to resentment.

Consider a situation in which someone who has enjoyed a high amount of autonomy suddenly finds themselves feeling limited in what decisions they can make, how they can live, or what goals they pursue by being part of the relationship. This loss of independence may cause tension and frustration as one works through the dichotomy of being a partner and yet longing for a sense of individuality.

In other cases, the loss of independence can lead to feelings of suffocation, jealousy, or even a longing for breathing space. This is where it becomes crucial for an individual to express their requirement for space, and a couple should be at the receiving end regarding respect for each other's autonomy.

You have to get real about losing your independence. Defining boundaries, respecting each other's need for space, and supporting what one does individually can reduce the imbalance in a relationship.

Discussing expectations, negotiating around where independence is vital, and discovering mutual compromises that enable both union and individual progress may benefit couples. It is essential that all the relationship members feel respected and that their identity and individuality can be expressed while remaining strong partners.

We must remember that relationships present challenges, and the form in which they affect individuals relies on personal dynamics. Overcoming these frustrations in a relationship and resolving them together comes down to communication, respect for one another, and both parties wanting to work on the hard stuff.

Every relationship is different as it depends on the personalities, experiences, and expectations of the individuals involved. Although every organization faces challenges and difficulties, the difference is often just how severe they are and their reach. A small block for one couple could be a real challenge for another.

One of the most essential ingredients in navigating relationship challenges is communication. Expressing feelings, concerns, and needs creates an understanding environment between partners. It allows couples to resolve conflicts, dig deeper into the root of an issue, and find common ground.

Equally important is mutual respect. A healthy relationship dynamic will allow for the individuality of each partner, respect a different point of view than your own, and honor one another's needs. Respecting emotional boundaries and personal space creates trust and understanding.

The stubbornness that keeps you working at it together through the messiness drives relationship resiliency. It takes both partners to work together, problem-solve, compromise, and continue to grow. Seeing challenges as opportunities for growth and learning reinforces the relationship connection when things get tough.

Relationships work when the groundwork is strong communication, respect for one another, and willingness to solve any problem. Couples who consciously grow in these things will be more capable of overcoming the inevitable challenges in any relationship, thereby creating a solid and satisfying union.

MASTERING FRUSTRATION

Why is it so complicated to deal with frustration in relationships?

Start an inventory of your feelings and what frustrates you. Identifying your emotional responses to whatever is going on between you is the first step to communicating effectively. Own your faults when warranted, and pardon your partner and yourself. Resentment keeps bitterness alive, while forgiveness fosters healing and helps the relationship evolve.

Practice deep transparency with your partner. Provide an arena for both people to speak openly (without fear of being judged) about their frustrations, worries, and needs. Tell them precisely what triggers the impatience and frustration. Knowing each other's trigger points allows you to manage and avoid situations likely to stir chaos together.

Talking properly and listening to one another is the key to understanding how both view things. Make the most of your time together to strengthen the emotional bond. Doing something fun and funny will help you make good memories together and mitigate frustrations.

Listen actively if you want to hear what your partner is trying to say. This means engaging with the whole being, validating your emotions, and being empathic. Listen without interrupting and attempt to imagine what they feel and go through.

Use "I" statements. When expressing your frustrations, use "I" statements and express how you feel instead of blaming or accusing your partner. For example, say, "I feel frustrated when..." instead of accusing, "You always..." This makes individual feelings palpable and tends not to set off defensiveness.

This will nurture patience in you when confronted with irritations, both yours and your partner's. Acknowledge that feelings are complicated and may need time to unravel. Give room for the issues to be sorted without rushing. Have empathy (understand your partner). Such a phrase evokes empathy and allows for building common ground so frustrations can be faced together.

View the frustrations as problems to solve together. Collaborate to solve problems instead of seeing each other as foes. Adopting this perspective helps partners feel like a team and bolsters their connections. Try seeking professional assistance if the frustrations continue and affect both parties in the relationship because it may take some time before one party settles down. A qualified therapist can help by offering guidance, communication strategies, and tools to work through challenges.

Realistically assess and modify expectations to match the reality of your relationship. You may have unrealistic expectations from your conversations, which can frustrate you. Practice identifying them and changing them to experience fulfillment in exchanges.

Finally, the best thing you can do is plan to be frustrated. Limiting your expectations of others only leads to failure, guilt, and sadness in your relationships. When one views all their annoyances as personal areas of development, they can weather the frustration and build a deeper, more meaningful relationship that will withstand whatever comes their way because it is built on reciprocity and trust.

MASTERING FRUSTRATION

Chapter 12

Dealing with Angry Children

While angry children are challenging to deal with, their emotions should not be treated lightly. A child with anger problems has many strong feelings, such as frustration, irritation, or anger. These can look like tantrums, meltdowns, defiance, or withdrawal. Developmentally Appropriateness—helping a child learn to handle anger acceptably is equally important as knowing they feel angry.

An angry child might overreact to small things. They often struggle to vocalize their feelings, so they act them out physically. They overreact if they feel misunderstood or unsupported and have problems with underlying issues, such as anxiety or stress, that may come from things other than school or social activities.

If you understand their anger triggers, can be a supportive and guiding presence in their lives, and are good at creating a safe environment, they are more likely to acquire practical emotional regulation abilities. When a child's anger appears overpowering or long-lasting, expert advice from a psychological intermediary with kids might assist.

Is there a pattern to the anger or something that seems to trigger the anger?

Sophie, a bright and joyful little seven-year-old girl, was looking forward to her birthday. It was a bike she had been practically dropping hints to get for weeks about, and even making a wish list of wants with the thing being brightly colored (and her favorite color) at a store.

The day finally arrived when Sophie could unwrap her birthday gifts, but the moment of joy changed in a second to sorrow. That bicycle was nowhere to be seen. So, she was given gifts such as books, art materials, and a board game.

Sophie beamed momentarily, and then her face settled into a pout. The disappointment was written all over her face. Then, the expectation of receiving that prized bike turned to disappointment and annoyance.

Understanding that Sophie was in a mood, her parents—both long-haul drivers during the week—reached out. Her mother said warmly, "We know you were hoping for the bike. These are just gifts we thought you'd really like... We'll do our best to make it up to you!"

Sophie, waving the rawness of her emotion away like a very literal storm cloud, felt angry. "But I wanted the bike!" she said. "It's not fair!"

Realizing her frustration, her parents saw a teachable moment session on the age-old life skill of expectation management and emotional expression. They told her that plans change sometimes, and people do not always get what they expect, but it is okay to be bummed or even a little mad. They told Sophie she was allowed to feel sad but assured her they would make sure they did something just for her birthday.

Sophie was slowly transitioning from anger into reflection about the unmet expectations, with her family discussing and processing their feelings. That afternoon, her parents took her on a surprise trip to the local park for a picnic and family bonding experience. While it was not the expected bicycle, they celebrated that day nonetheless because they knew how to handle disappointment and had other ways of celebrating.

Just as adults can feel angry for many different reasons, so can children. Parents, caregivers, and educators must understand children's anger sources to provide emotional support and teach them healthy ways to deal with their emotions. Children get angry, but here are some common triggers of that anger:

Kids tend to mimic adult and peer behavior. If they see adults mismanaging their anger, they may repeat those behaviors when confronted with adversity.

For some children, childhood trouble and self-control problems often lead to difficulty controlling anger appropriately. Individual character and maturation may affect this.

For instance, children who have chronic anger might be struggling with underlying mood disorders, anxiety, or other mental health issues. These are challenges that may require professional help to solve.

Competition between siblings, jealousy over attention and belongings, or seeming favoritism can result in anger. When their emotions are not expressed, children develop a strong sense of anger that can be exhibited outward.

Anger can be aroused when children have social problems, such as disagreements with friends, rejection, and being excluded from a group. Social dynamics can be tricky; there are sides or cliques, and expression of emotion is often told just to put a smile on!

Failing to reach a goal, handle a challenge, or do something suitable can be frustrating, and this may come out as anger in kids who don't have the coping abilities that adults do. Kids can become grumpy or angry when they're hungry, tired, sick, or in physical pain. They may not always have the ability to express their needs.

Children—particularly younger ones—get angry when an aspect of their environment or situation makes them feel out of control. This may happen when routines change or in situations where they feel helpless. The journey can become increasingly more challenging if a child has difficulty completing academic tasks and feels angry or frustrated due to overwhelming learning challenges. Academic struggles may feel like a threat to their competence.

Anger can also be a response to fear or anxiety, which children often feel. Feeling angry is usually a way of coping with the intense feelings that arise from new experiences, being away from caregivers (which can be frightening in and of itself), or fear of the unknown.

Children become angry when expectations are not fulfilled, or desires are opposed. This may happen when we do not get our favorite toy or do not succeed in something. Another reason anger is a typical response for children is when their opinions, needs, or emotions are belittled by an adult (including their peers).

By recognizing these different sources of anger in children, caregivers and educators can offer specific guidance on coping skills and create an environment that promotes positive emotional health and expression.

How to Handle Angry Kids

When a child is mad, you must keep calm. Your calm will make them feel safe and secure. Identify their feelings—You can say, "I see that you are angry." This will make them feel that their situation is taken seriously, so you respect what they are going through.

Acknowledge their frustration with something like, "I get it. This makes the child feel that their emotions are understood and more genuine as they do not feel alone. Urge them to say how they feel. Use open-ended questions such as: "Can you explain what is wrong?" and listen attentively.

Teach your kids good ways to cope with frustration, including calming methods like breathing techniques, counting to ten, or possibly a break. Let them understand that feeling frustrated is okay, but also help them know how to express it correctly. Acts of aggression or verbal abuse are unacceptable.

Behavioral Learning: Children observe those who care for them. Teach them frustration management through your actions. Do not punish or give harsh consequences for venting displeasure. Instead, create an environment to communicate and solve problems.

Help kids problem-solve through their frustration. Say, "How might we improve this?" and involve them in the solutions. Acknowledge and celebrate when children do well controlling their frustration. They are more likely to pursue and utilize other healthy coping methods when we reinforce that behavior.

Handling upset kids is one of the more significant components of conquering home and family frustration. When you offer them the tools to navigate their emotions and a gentle helping hand, you set them on course for emotional resilience and life skills. Nurturing children's emotional well-being is a crucial part of managing frustration at home because it will change how you relate to the younger ones, modeling how to deal with adverse circumstances faced in life.

Chapter 13

Handling Your Angry Teenager

Adolescence is a testy time in one's life, and parents, caregivers, and mentors must all learn how to deal with angry teenagers. This is a period of great physical and mental transition for these youngsters. They're discovering independence, identity, and new challenges. Their path can be littered with frustration and anger.

As a 16-year-old high school student, Emma was always headstrong and independent. Recently, her parents—especially her mother, Sarah—noticed an uptick in defiance regarding curfew. There was a household rule—be in by 10:00 PM on school nights.

One night, at 11:30 PM, Emma walked in the door long after her curfew. In the living room, Sarah sat waiting for her, worried and angry.

Sarah: "Oh, Emma, do you know what time it is? We established a curfew, and these are the rules."

Emma [rolling her eyes]: "Whatever, Mom. Everyone stays out

late."

Sarah, half concerned, half angry: "It is a big deal. I need to know that you are safe, and we create rules for a reason. Where were you? Why didn't you text or call?"

Emma: "Chill, Mom—like, come on, ugh. I was chillin' with friends. Nothing terrible happened."

Sarah, exhaling: "Emma, this isn't just me 'chilling.' It is a matter of accountability and dialogue. We need to trust each other."

Emma: "Big deal. It's just curfew. I can take care of myself."

Sarah recognized that if she did not have a more constructive conversation, she would not be able to talk further or go to the principal's office, so she decided to pick her battles as well.

Sarah: "Emma, I get you want your freedom and understand, but what about being a bit wiser with how much freedom you have? I suggest an appropriate curfew and suggestions on how we can communicate better. It's a delicate balance between being an adult and our desire to know you're safe."

Emma, reluctant but opening up: "Okay, but I don't want a freaking nine o'clock curfew."

Over the next few days, Sarah and Emma discussed curfews, trust, and communication several times. Eventually, the two sides found a mutually agreeable compromise.

Clashes between parents and teenagers about rules versus

independence in adolescence are hardly surprising, given different personalities, family circumstances, and cultural influences. Adolescents undergo a developmental stage of pursuing independence, exploration, identity, and autonomy.

Common areas of conflict between parents and kids include curfew, screen time, socializing, academic workload, personal space, and privacy. Other issues involve clothing and appearance, developing responsibility through chores and jobs, financial independence, dating, romantic relationships, and decision-making—learning to push boundaries before adulthood.

Negotiating curfews and bedtimes have become a contention because teenagers now want more freedom in managing both. From phones and computers to video games, there may be arguments over how much screen time teenagers use.

Socializing with friends can become a battle of wills between parents and teenagers who may want to go to parties, sleepovers, or hang out at the mall—not to mention stay up late. This type of conflict may involve how your child studies, what you expect from them academically, and how much time they spend on schoolwork versus their other activities.

As adolescent children, teens often want greater privacy, and battles may stem over boundaries about private space, private affairs, and the rights to privacy in areas of their lives. Conflicts over ideas on dress and style can put parents and teens at odds with each other.

When parents push teens to work hard at home, arguments can erupt over responsibilities and chores. When teenagers work their first jobs or want to earn money, tensions can also build around earning and spending money.

Different expectations can lead to tension in dating and romantic relationships during adolescence. Whether at home or school, teens want more freedom to make decisions, and that naturally creates friction over everything from hairstyles and clothing to college or a career path.

Tensions are a standard component of the parent-teen dynamic during puberty. They can be viewed as moments of growth, learning, and negotiating. While teen rebellion can lead to conflict, it is also a normal part of growing into adulthood. And if handled well through good communication skills, respect for one another, and compromise, it can help build a parent-teen relationship that lasts through this challenging but critical phase of development. However, how this plays out in many families is a tug of war between your teen wanting independence and you, as a parent, setting the boundaries.

Tips for Managing an Angry Teenager

Dealing with an angry teenager means you must remain calm, be patient, and understand that anger cannot be fixed in one day.

Promote transparent communication. Encourage an open dialogue between parents and teens where they feel free to voice their opinions, ideas, feelings, or concerns without fear of criticism. When teenagers talk, you have to be completely quiet and relaxed. Let them express their anger, and without interruption, encourage full expression of feelings. Even in disagreement, reflect on their feelings to show empathy. If nothing else, put yourself in the teenager's shoes and remember what it was like to go through that turmoil of feelings. Acknowledge their feelings: This must be frustrating for you. Apologize for their feelings and let them know that their feelings matter. While you share your need as a parent, recognize their desire for independence and freedom.

Instead of needing to control all discourse, show healthy conflict resolution—practice modeling good communication and problem-solving skills between the two most significant aspects of your life. Teach teens how to deal with conflict positively. Establish a space that allows your teen to express what they are angry about. Please encourage them to open up about what bothers them and listen attentively.

Talk about the repercussions of specific actions, and explain to a teen why you have the rules you do. This can help them develop a sense of responsibility and accountability for what they do. Attack the problem, not the person. Do not accuse your teenager of being like they are. Stop doing this and instead tackle the issue and talk about solutions. Teach coping strategies—teaching your teen some coping skills for frustration is a great idea. These could be exercising, hobbies, or confiding in a friend.

Avoid power struggles, especially as teenagers seek independence. Offer choices and compromise when possible, aiming for solutions that protect both sides. Provide freedom while maintaining guidance. Teens, even those engaging in risky behavior, need structure. Set clear expectations, explain the reasoning behind rules, and involve them in the process, making it more likely they'll follow through.

Take a gradual approach to granting more independence as they prove responsible. That may put them more in charge of their decision-making and let them reap the outcomes of their choices within safe limits. Celebrate the successes and positive behavior. When teens make good decisions or act responsibly, acknowledge and commend their efforts.

As teens assert their independence, they'll want space, personal privacy, and time alone—be sure to respect the teenager's desire for it. A sound parent-child relationship is mainly built on trust. Set the appropriate boundaries while navigating to maintain their independence, yet still encourage some level of parenting.

If your teen's anger is long-term, extreme, or hurting them or someone else, ask a therapist or counselor for help. Professional help will add more tools and guidance for parents and teenagers.

Remember that resolving clashes is a process and may take some time. Establishing the ability to lean into trust, empathy, and communication will produce a better functioning parent-teen dynamic in those tumultuous teen years.

Dealing with an angry teenager is one step toward frustration mastery. These strategies and being available to support during such a disruptive period will enable your adolescent to build emotional strength and resilience. This is a journey into uncharted territory for both parents and teens. Remember, no one survives this part intact.

Chapter 14

Navigating the Financial Challenges

Financial frustration is an emotion that causes you to feel upset or disappointed when facing challenges, difficulties, unmet goals, and expectations in your finances. This psychological reaction to financial pressure can take different forms depending on individual situations, beliefs, and relationships to money.

Income-related issues seem to affect many people, but their consequences go beyond money and impact different areas of daily living. Lack of money, income, job loss, and uncertainty aren't just about the balance in the bank account—they also bring emotional and psychological challenges.

Frustration kicks in when people discover they are making less than what is needed to pay for their essentials and live a decent life. This economic hardship can be a constant battle to pay for basic expenses, including rent, utilities, food, and health care. Not participating in elements that make life worth living can add further frustration, as people may feel restricted from social, cultural, or leisure activities.

Along with the immediate financial pressure, an unexpected job loss stirs up a range of hurdles we tend not to recognize. In addition to the stress of negotiating their way through unemployment, people may feel an even more profound frustration associated with losing the identity, structure, and stability that their jobs provide. Lack of income disrupts the ability to pay bills, but it also impairs self-esteem and identity, creating a compound trauma.

Having an unpredictable financial situation will wear you out emotionally. The constant struggle of contrast due to an unsteady income, an on-and-off job, or even freelancing can create a lack of patience. People struggle to prepare for the future, make long-term financial decisions, or create a stable base for themselves and their families.

If someone has trouble earning a general income, panic might set in as they try to figure out how to pay the rent next month, while others feel more irritated by their current situation because their work dream can not begin due to this income challenge. Societal expectations and pressures exacerbate these frustrations and create additional obstacles to mental and emotional well-being. The burden of debt can be frustrating — bills, the stress of spending money, or the obligation to pay back these bills; all very annoying when it seems too much or unworkable.

As bad as it sounds, even things like medical bills and car repairs can be frustrating if people aren't prepared to deal with them financially. Hustling for a job or working in grunt positions is frustrating, and people cannot reach their career and financial dreams.

Failing to reach financial targets like buying a house, schooling, or aging gracefully can be difficult on the soul and only add frustration. For anyone who has seen their investment value reduced through poor investment returns or market movement, it can result in anger.

So when prices are up and their cost of living skyrockets, life can seem frustrating when they realize their income is not increasing in line with inflation (which everybody hates to hear). If one partner earns significantly more than the other, frustration may arise based on perceived financial disparity and inequities regarding how money is managed.

Comparing yourself to others and getting frustrated by your own lack of prosperity. Partial ignorance of financial fundamentals leads one to feel frustrated about not being able to make sound finance-related decisions.

Recessions or economic downturns trigger financial anxiety and frustration as they enter an unknown economic landscape. Financial issues can be cumbersome for many of us and can lead to a lot of stress, lack of sleep, and anxiety. Handling the budget gaps requires handling a fiscal challenge with an upbeat and open-minded approach. To get through the challenges of a strict budget, here are some essential strategies:

Tackling income problems requires a holistic, multi-pronged approach that involves more than just money. It includes finance, building skills, and developing emotional resilience. By introducing practical approaches like searching for extra income, learning fresh skills, and establishing a reasonable budget, one can contend with the entanglement of financial disappointment and work hard towards a more secure and satisfying economic future.

How do you get away from your money problems?
Providing for basic needs is part of financial freedom; all with a fixed income can do this. By carefully managing budgets, minimizing non-essential expenditures, and developing a sustainable economic plan, they can fund housing with all necessary utilities, groceries, and healthcare without constantly

stress-testing their capacity to last the month.

Choosing this path to freedom is about knowing where you want to be, having a goal, taking a good direction, and being willing and determined to go through the process. For people measured by the vagaries of fixed incomes, financial freedom comes down to making prudent moves, escaping debt prison, covering essentials without stress, and finally enjoying their organic life. This journey is more significant than money, representing hope and empowerment.

Strategic planning is the compass that points you in the right direction through the complex landscape of financial freedom. It's a comprehensive evaluation of your financial state, setting achievable objectives and a blueprint guiding your journey to financial freedom. Strategic planning is a bespoke framework that accounts for the fundamental nature of fixed incomes.

The Art of Personal Finance:
Personal finance is the term that refers to an individual's or a household's financial activities—the management of personal finances, including budgeting, saving, investing, and applying for loans. It encompasses determining how to make your money work for you at your best by planning how to spend, pay off debt, save for things like college or retirement, and slowly invest in

wealth-building. Personal finance is the entire process of how you manage your money, including saving and spending. Financial wellness includes various aspects associated with economic well-being and is intended to maximize the efficiency of monetary resources in meeting both short-term and long-term financial goals.

Inflation is a more stealthy but just as damaging enemy of retirees living off a fixed income. Believed by many to be the "silent killer" of consumer behavior, this economic phenomenon subversively creeps into the wallets of those on a fixed income. Amid an overall economy in which the cost of living creeps ever higher, the money once produced by a fixed income steadily buys less and less, making for a bleak financial scene.

As inflation absurdly marches forward, those on fixed incomes are left riding the tightrope of a work-life balancing act. Inflation is the gradual but insatiable rise in the cost of goods and services, robbing millions of individuals on fixed incomes or pensions of their right to maintain a lifestyle they earned. From food staples to more extensive purchase obligations, a relentless cost increase leads to a minefield of financial impacts.

A fixed income can be likened to a shrinking reservoir of purchasing power, leaving individuals scrambling to afford

MASTERING FRUSTRATION

necessities. The decisions get a bit complicated, which requires a thoughtful approach to financial decision-making. Every expense is scrutinized as people stretch every dollar—rising inflation, housing costs, groceries, and countless other expenses make it harder to make ends meet.

Inflation in several developed countries is proving to be a formidable opponent that cannot go unchallenged, leading people to rethink their financial approaches while putting another strategy into place to protect themselves against its corrosive effects. Such a time, therefore, is ripe for searching avenues that not only prevent the burdensome effects of climbing prices from cutting into fixed incomes but even make it resilient to this silent yet deadly enemy in the economy.

In the world we live in today, where inflation continues to put pressure on us with a fixed income, it is essential to plan strategically, diversify investments, and adapt continuously to be fortified against the erosive effects of this force of nature. Awareness of the underlying motivations can give way to more sound decision-making, leading you to greater financial security that either outperforms inflation or insulates its impact from your personal life.

Managing debt on a fixed income becomes a constant struggle, especially for those without fluctuating earnings. It creates a relentless tug-of-war with expenses, weighing heavily on aspirations and reminding them of looming repayments that drain hope for a better life.

For those on pensions, working their budget around paid debt can be like dragging a millstone from month to month. This chain that presents itself as flimsy at best gets tighter over time, making it difficult to enjoy what you worked for. The time when many want to reap the benefits of work becomes a never-ending balancing act of debt commitments, leaving only room for personal goals and ambitions.

Debt is more than a financial burden; it lodges itself into other parts of people's lives. It influences how much they can save for self-development, take up hobbies, or even spend on things they enjoy doing and value the most. This unending awareness of the bills needing to be paid causes constant stress, which affects well-being and outweighs the feel-good euphoria that should accompany receiving a fixed income.

Escaping the jaws of debt is a very strategic and intentional process. This means having a strategy to pay down and ultimately eliminate the oppressive debt burden, not just making monthly payments. Finding freedom from debt is significant for taking the initial step towards awareness of economic life and directing free resources towards high-monetization activities.

Managing essential bills like rent, lights, and food becomes a dangerous game of balance—one that necessitates walking on eggshells and inching carefully forward one step at a time. Those with no choice but to work through the often brutal realities of cash on a limited income know this fear well—the fear of being unable to meet these basic needs for survival and dignity looms above, adding an extra layer of hardship to their financial struggles.

For seniors with a fixed income, everyday life puts automatic stress on their financial resources. Housing is that bedrock of security, absorption of quite a share of the budget, and little allowance for other essentials. Then there are the utilities, adding to a growing pile of pressure as people everywhere try to hang on to some semblance of comfort and security within their budgets. Groceries are one of the few bills that require detailed line-by-line evaluation due to their tangible nature.

In financially challenging times, people fear not having access to basic needs and try to make do. This constant worry serves as a reminder of instability, always looming overhead. As they tally how many times 100 euros might stretch in their monthly groceries, the unsettling belief that a limit is approaching begins to take hold. Not only does this fear undermine economic security, but it compromises the quality of life.

The first step is to create a budget that carefully distributes available resources among essentials. If we go about things granularly—from housing to groceries—nothing will go unattended.

It is essential to spot the areas where you can trim down costs without compromising necessities. As time passes, and the sum of these minor tweaks is considered, they can realistically add up to eliminating our ability to satisfy basic needs, which is possible without costing a fortune.

Community resources and aid programs may come in handy during financial stress. Whether you need housing assistance, food programs, or other resources, they can be a lifeline for those facing challenges.

Ironically, the path to financial freedom often lies in defeating the most significant enemy: DEBT. Once people have their monthly incomes secured by making a budget, the following crucial action they need to take is to find successful ways of paying off debt, which will put them on track to take charge of their financial fates. In this guide, we will cover two effective strategies—the Snowball Method and the Avalanche Method—approaches to paying off debts that can help you on your journey toward a debt-free life.

The Snowball Method:
The Snowball Method is a debt repayment strategy that recommends beginning with the smallest debts before working your way up to the largest. The psychological logic behind this technique is similar to pushing a snowball down a hill: The motivation and momentum gained in paying off one debt make you more likely to tackle the next.

Paying off small debts first gives a mental victory, providing a feeling of progress and accomplishment. People feel real wins as they see their debts go down. Such validation acts as a catalyst, driving them to continue paying off their debts.

While The Snowball Method seems numerical, it is all about behavior. Achieving milestones early in the process creates positive incentives that help ensure commitment to getting out of debt. This is an excellent approach if you are motivated by physical markers.

Avalanche Method:

The second method, which is analytical and oriented towards numbers, is called the Avalanche Method. With this method, you first aim to pay off the debts with the highest interest rates to save money in the long run. The Avalanche Method will not give you those quick psychological wins that may help motivate you at first, like the Snowball Method, but it is better for more game time and a more financially sound approach.

The central concept behind the Avalanche Method is to eliminate debts with the highest interest rates first. Doing so will help you minimize the total interest charged, saving you more money as you pay your debt over time. This principle is based on an economic-saving strategy that aims to achieve the best quality at the lowest price.

The Avalanche Method may not offer the same instant gratification as the Snowball Method, but it caters to anyone looking to maximize their money over time. Removing high-interest debt increases your chances of paying off the remaining debts as quickly as possible, reducing their total cost over time.

Choosing the Right Strategy:
Whether the Snowball vs. Avalanche Method is better for you depends on your desire, financial situation, and psychology. Perhaps the Snowball Method appeals to those whose mantra

centers around small victories and feel-good kicks in the pants. Alternatively, it simply refers to a preference for strategic effectiveness and more savings via an avalanche method.

The important thing is not to be flummoxed but buoyed when traversing through the arena of debt repayment. Substantial successes with both methods prove the value of a strategy that works for you based on personal preferences and what motivates you. Regardless of their direction, the journey to financial freedom will move forward, only needing that first intentional step to set them down a path toward living free of debt and in control over money.

Establishing a Realistic Budget: Setting Your Balance
When living on a fixed income, the first step in managing finances is preparing an accurate budget. A budget functions like a map, directing you to where your scarce resources should be going and how you can make wise financial decisions. In this guide, we explore the foundational pillars of budgeting—needs vs. wants—and how to discover areas where you can optimize your expenses.

Learning the difference between wants and needs is the key to designing an accurate budget. Needs include necessities to sustain a reliable and stable life, including housing, utilities, food, and personal health. On the contrary, wants are non-essential expenditures that improve lifestyle but are not necessary for survival.

The first step is to allocate money for essential needs before spending it on unimportant things. This is a way for people to protect their basic needs like shelter, heat, and water. Establishing this level of financial footing provides the strong groundwork for addressing any further discretionary spending.

After the requirements are met, the next stage of budgeting is to recognize which expenses can be reduced. Making tweaks across different aspects of spending will accumulate savings over time. Budgeting is most definitely not about deprivation; it is about making the most of your money so as to match your spending with your financial goals.

Recurring expenses, like subscriptions, regular dining out, or spur-of-the-moment buys, can be broken down and optimized as needed. Examining each expense category with a critical eye allows one to find potential areas of savings while still maintaining one's overall quality of life.

A few decimal places were added here, adding up to some substantial dollars over time. From bargaining bills and opting for the cheapest substitutes to limiting non-essential purchases, each of these minor adjustments facilitates the establishment of a budget that is sustainable and equally realistic in the context of low incomes.

A Holistic Approach to Budgeting:
A realistic budget is a dynamic document that changes with the circumstances. It consists of a global approach considering immediate cash flow and long-term objectives. A realistic budget gives people the information and tools to spend wisely, allocate scarce resources judiciously, and build sustainable financial ecosystems.

Beyond discussing needs vs. wants, a reasonable budget should also set money aside for an emergency fund. This is a financial safety net to cover unexpected expenses and soften the blow if shit goes sideways.

A realistic budget can help control spending to align with bigger financial goals. More importantly, if you are looking to save towards a future investment, maybe building an emergency fund or paying down debts, the budget becomes a tactical guide that helps make sure financial dreams come true.

Emergency Fund Building:

An emergency fund is one of the key threads of financial planning. Currently, this financial reservoir provides individuals who rely on fixed incomes with strength in the midst of uncertainty, acting as a net that catches any expected expenses and prevents them from creating a massive black cloud over their finances.

The emergency fund is more than just a financial tool; it is strategic protection against life's unforeseen circumstances. It is a pot of money that has been placed aside for unexpected and immediate bills that can throw financial equilibrium out of balance.

No one can predict life, and just like that, you will find out about some medical emergency or your house needs an instant repair, forcing you to spend thousands unexpectedly. Having an emergency fund is like having a shield that protects against the unforeseen things that happen in life, giving people the room to deal with these unexpected challenges without upsetting their entire financial status.

For many people, especially those who rely on fixed income, unexpected expenses can have a profound financial effect. These unexpected events disrupt budgets that have been in the works for months and more, result in debt, and exacerbate the hardship of economic stress, all without an emergency fund. So, building an emergency fund is a proactive way to account for these potential derailers so you have a good measuring stick against what financial control looks like.

Financial Resilience — The Foundation for the Future:
One common finance rule involves the 70/30 principle, which means allocating 70% of your income to expenses and saving or investing only the remaining 30%. This ensures that a large slice of income is reserved for essentials and investment efforts, thus creating security and stability—a simple method to keep track of money, widely adopted as a personal finance management system.

The 70/30 rule is essentially a simplified version of the 50/30/20 rule, which Elizabeth Warren and Amelia Warren Tyagi made famous in their book All Your Worth: The Ultimate Lifetime Money Plan. Under the 50/30/20 rule, finances are divided into three areas: needs (50%), wants (30%), savings and debt repayment (20%). The 70/30 rule is a variant more oriented toward essential and savings issues.

This is how the 70/30 rule is most often implemented:
Factor in your income—salary, including other sources of income, for example, rental yields (after tax). Invest 70% of your

after-tax income in living expenses, including rent or mortgage, utilities, food, transportation, insurance, and other needed bills.

Then, take the rest of the 30% based on your thoughts: (a). Donations, Capital-Asset Investment, and Saving. (b). OR (c), emergency reserve, pension and individual hobbies, saving for emergencies, debt pay, entertainment/dining. This means you can further split the other 30% portion into savings for emergencies, retirement, and non-essential discretionary expenses such as entertainment, dining out, or personal hobbies.

The 70/30 rule can be essential but should be adjusted according to individual cases. If your living costs are high, you may need to devote more than 70% to needs versus wants—or vice versa; if your living costs are low, this may create some wiggle room about being able to fund savings or non-essentials. Reassess your budget regularly and adjust according to changes in income, outgoings, or financial objectives. That is why the rule should be somewhat flexible depending on your circumstances.

Please keep in mind that the 70/30 rule is just a guideline, and your financial conditions may differ. For some people, saving aggressively may be more desirable, while for others who are facing high housing costs or medical bills, a more significant percentage may go to living expenses. The beauty of this one is that it can be tailored to your budget and based on personal goals, lifestyle habits, and life stages.

Build a savings account for an emergency:
Creating an emergency fund is not a desire but rather one of the principles of financial strength. This means saving money specifically for emergencies intentionally and consistently. Following these principles can help you create an adequate emergency fund and keep it intact.

An emergency fund can only be built up through consistent deposits, even tiny amounts. As with the Sinking Fund, even if you can only put away a small sum each month or a percentage of your income, be it as low as 10-15% at times, consistency is key! Over time, it adds up.

An emergency fund does not have a standard amount; it depends on the individual's situation. The amount will vary based on several factors, including monthly spending requirements, income volatility, and individual risk appetite. Crafting the fund according to individual requirements helps to fulfill financial goals and meet important obligations.

An emergency fund should be on hand to draw from in emergencies, but it still needs to be separate from the funds you can access for daily spending. This separation helps protect the fund from being used for anything other than a true emergency.

An emergency fund is so much more than just money in the bank. It gives people confidence because they know they have financial protection against unexpected events. It helps alleviate the pressures of uncertainty, removing tendencies to worry about upcoming expenses as you manage your long-term financial goals.

Put simply, building an emergency fund is buying yourself a little peace of mind. It changes the unavoidability of life's unknowns. Sustainable living on a fixed income helps strengthen your financial resilience by establishing an emergency fund so you can approach the future more confidently, knowing that you have built a strong safety net to catch any unforeseen emergencies.

Request for Expert Opinion:
Seeking professional assistance is a key piece of advice in financial management when facing the challenges of fixed incomes. Getting in touch with a financial advisor is one of the best strategies for receiving personalized guidance and developing actionable plans that pave the road to financial health, debt reduction, and preparation for the future.

MASTERING FRUSTRATION

A financial advisor is an individual with good experience and the knowledge and skills to provide assistance in personal finance. It's not just about the numbers; it'll be about knowing personal situations, financial goals, and discrimination within fixed incomes.

The most significant advantage you may enjoy by hiring a professional is that they can give you tailored advice on handling fixed incomes. Financial advisors will identify each client's best circumstances, including income stability, spending patterns, and time horizons. That means your recommendations are tailored for you and address all the unique needs and challenges with these fixed incomes.

Financial advisors can also help those who are in debt pay it off or get free of it. Their insights can guide individuals on how to balance debt reduction with the need for a repayment plan, negotiate terms with creditors, and prioritize expenses during the process.

Future planning is not just about financial resources. Financial advisors help create long-term strategies, such as retirement planning and investment management. This insight empowers people to make wise choices that align with their financial goals, paving the way for a stable and prosperous tomorrow.

The Process of Seeking Professional Guidance:
The process of engaging a professional financial advisor is fairly methodical in approach—one that seeks to maximize the advantages of such a dynamic.

It usually starts with a preliminary meeting in which prospective clients describe their needs, goals, changes, and existing situations. The advisor must have a complete picture of the client's financial ecosystem.

Financial advisors will thoroughly evaluate the client's financial situation, including sources of income, expenses, debts, and assets. This comprehensive analysis serves as a foundation for personalized suggestions and solutions.

Following this evaluation, advisors create a personalized financial plan that meets clients' immediate needs and prepares for long-term planning. It takes money to make money, but not having a lot of it also doesn't have to stop you from creating a plan that keeps your eyes on the prize as you strive for financial stability, pay off debt, and look toward building a future.

Well, working with a financial advisor is usually a long-term relationship in which your adviser reviews and modifies your financial plan as things change. This collaborative methodology ensures that the financial tactics stay pliant and ever-responsive to shifting prerequisites and goals.

This, in turn, allows people to make sound and strategic financial decisions by seeking professional assistance. A financial advisor plays the same role; their expertise becomes a compass that contains fixed incomes, debt management, and future planning. By leveraging this treasure trove of experience, even the most confused entities can feel confident in traversing their financial fields with a much-needed, life-long guiding hand to provide them with advice, methods of solutions, and support on their journey of achieving financial health.

Core Content Investing in the Financial Markets:
The art of the investment play is a cornerstone in personal finance, particularly when it comes to optimally using inflexible incomes for long-term benefit. Wise investing is a careful examination of opportunities that fit your risk tolerance and goals, along with the bonus of diversification to produce a portfolio that weathers economic cycles.

Make your investments wisely by making strategic investment decisions that factor in individual financial situation, risk appetite, and long-term ambitions. Investors who have recently started to assess investments should be aware of the following:

Everyone has a different risk tolerance—the degree of risk one is willing to accept regarding investment uncertainty. Before entering investment opportunities, it is essential to evaluate one's risk tolerance. This awareness of oneself helps lay the groundwork for conscious decisions based on comfort.

Investing in the stock market—Financial goals are of the utmost importance when choosing an investment. Be it retirement, home purchase, or any other milestones, investing according to specific goals ensures that the strategies and instruments help achieve those aspirations.

On the other hand, diversification is an investment strategy that involves dispersing capital across various asset classes, sectors, or geographies. This risk management approach reduces the overall portfolio's pain from investments that perform poorly. By diversifying, investors can smooth out the ups and downs caused by economic conditions or business cycles and increase the stability of their portfolios.

The investment world is also an enticing field with many options, but for any type of venture, investors should be wise. What are common avenues for investment exploration?

Stocks signify your ownership in a company, which could result in capital appreciation. Successful stock investing requires understanding the stock market, individual companies, and economic conditions.

A bond is an interest-bearing or periodic debt security that comes with the return of principal at maturity. They are lower risk than stocks and can earn steady income over time.

Real estate investment means buying a property with the hope that it will appreciate or generate rental income. It is a tangible asset and can add diversification to an investment portfolio.

These funds gather money from many different investors to buy a wide range of individual stocks, bonds, or other assets. Exchange-traded funds (ETFs) and mutual funds offer diversification and managed funds.

Money was invested in the 401(k)s or IRAs: Retirement accounts are often tax-deductible, and investing for the long term is a great way to achieve retirement goals.

Managing Risks and Constant Evaluation
Responsible investing requires risk management and continual

assessment. It is essential to periodically review the investment portfolio for alignment with goals, risk tolerance, and market conditions. Changes in personal situations or the economy might require adjustment.

Having an emergency fund is paramount, so before investing, ensure that you have created and will maintain one. A contingency fund acts as a safety net for your financial plan so that any unforeseen expenses can be paid without derailing your investment plans.

Consultation with financial experts, such as investment advisors, can be invaluable to your decision-making process. With the proper professional guidance, people can understand how best to proceed based on their financial situation.

To cut a long story short, investment is equal parts planning, equal parts risk management, and just as many learning experiences along the way. With capital sinks, risk tolerance levels, and diversification strategies aligned to long-term goals, income-restricted stakeholders will be equipped to engage with the financial markets without concern. The path to achieving financial independence is not one followed in a sprint. Still, from the outside looking in, rather than what appears as an elaborate chess game, each investment move leads you closer to your checkmate—a comfortable life where you no longer have to work for money.

Financial Literacy: The Most Powerful Destroyer
In the dynamic field of personal finance, pursuing ongoing education is a valuable asset for individuals managing their limited income. Constantly reading about personal finance topics, new investment ideas, and economic events is more than just a good idea—it should be a strategic necessity that protects each individual's ability to change their financial plans as needed to assure financial success for life.

Continuous learning in personal finance is more than just knowledge—it is about an ongoing process of empowerment and adaptability. The following are reasons why and how continuous solid learning can help a person maximize their financial success:

Economic landscapes are fluid, with tides and trends that can influence personal finances. Continuous learning, also known as lifelong learning, allows people to be aware of new economic happenings and how these changes require alterations to their financial plans. An informed person is equipped to go with the tides of the financial world, be it changes in interest rates, market trends, or regulatory fluctuations.

Investments are an intricate space with wide avenues continuously coming up. By keeping pace with new investment trends, risk management techniques, and other innovations in financial instruments, continuous education also contributes to ensuring that it is aware of everything. They can use this information to maximize their investments and look for opportunities that meet their goals and peace of mind.

Financial literacy is the basis of sound decision-making in personal finance. A commitment to continuous learning also proves valuable for financial literacy, as it helps us better understand budgeting, debt management, retirement planning, and much more. A person who knows the facts is in the correct position to make tactical decisions that will contribute to long-term financial success.

Strategies to Keep Learning:

Continuous learning is a street in both directions: it means actively seeking knowledge from many sources. Below are tips to encourage continual financial literacy:

Read various forms of financial literature, such as books, articles, and good financial media. Look for topics related to your current financial situation or that you want to learn more about.

Engage in workshops, web-based video courses, and other educational events run by authorities and establishments in the financial field. These are just platforms to learn from experts, follow along as your professionals speak and answer questions, and keep up with trends in personal finance.

Many online websites offer personal finance, investing, and associated courses with certification. These courses offer a guided learning experience and an opportunity to gain certifications.

Links with finance professionals, such as financial advisors or investment experts, give access to personalized advice and insights. Networking will give you a bird's-eye view and enable your practical finance acumen.

Personal finance education is a lifelong journey that requires curiosity, open-mindedness, and flexibility as the world of finance evolves. The bottom line is that when fixed-income individuals develop an attitude of lifelong learning, they can bolster their financial skills and be one step ahead in a changing financial landscape. This is an ongoing journey of empowerment, and every little you learn helps grow into a bedrock of economic freedom that will last for generations.

At the center of this journey is a commitment to financial freedom. This requires an active decision to favor long-term ambitions over current pleasures. It is about facing the reality of fixed incomes head-on and adopting a forward-thinking attitude that searches for answers and areas to expand.

Finding financial freedom is not just about trying to get rich; it is a path leading to overall prosperity. Economic independence, however, is not just about money; it also includes your emotional health to a certain extent. FWF does encompass the absence of financial stress and fear, along with making choices that empower us to lead our lives based on what we value and aspire to.

Finally, achieving financial freedom is an empowering journey that anyone on a fixed income can undertake—just be smart about it! With these tips, such as following the advice of experts, getting out of debt, fulfilling basic needs, and living with meaning, it is possible to walk on the way to prosperity and feel the effects of financial liberation. While the road to financial freedom may come with its challenges, dedication, and endurance, it enables us not just to dream of a future free from wage slavery but also to make it tangible.

Chapter 15

Frustration Management Techniques

Fundamental frustration management techniques are essential tools in your emotional toolbox, designed to help you manage frustration and maintain control over your emotions. These practices build resilience, enhance self-awareness, and encourage a more positive response during tough times. So let us take a look at these must-have tools:

Deep breathing—A simple but effective method to control the frustration. In those instances, you feel irritation when it starts to rise, so take a moment and breathe deeply. Then, count for two to four seconds, holding your breath and exhaling slowly. This can help settle your nervous system, respond, and visualize in the heat. Breathing is a way for our idle mind to focus. When someone takes a deep breath and exhales intentionally, it brings a focus point that will calm your mind and take your attention away from distractions.

When we breathe deeply, our bodies turn on the parasympathetic nervous system—called the "rest and digest" system. The result is the opposite of the stress response: The balanced sympathetic nervous system creates a feeling of peace and relaxation. Deep breaths tend to be slow and controlled, which tells the body that it is safe enough to move into a more restful state.

Deep Breathing Exercise
Breathe deeply through your nose, concentrating on filling your diaphragm rather than primarily using your chest. Notice how your stomach flares as you inhale, feeling the breath gently washing through your lungs.

Allow the breath to continue, filling your chest. This slow expansion captures all the air in your lungs and creates fullness and oxygen.

Inhale through your nose and release slowly out of your mouth. With each exhale, visualize releasing tension, stress, negativity, or frustration. Release negative energy and emotion with the breath.

Let go of the thoughts you know aggravate your annoyance as you breathe out. Visualize those thoughts blowing away with the out-breath, creating a mental space of calmness by emptying your mind of worries and concerns.

Taking deep breaths lowers stress, gradually reducing anxiety levels. It initiates the relaxation response that reduces cortisol levels (the stress hormone) and releases physical symptoms of stress. This, in return, adds to the feeling of equilibrium in the mind and heart.

Meditating helps improve your lungs by regularly practicing deep breathing. This encourages the diaphragm to move fully, allowing for an effective exchange of gas (oxygen and carbon dioxide). It can benefit people who tend to breathe shallowly when stressed out.

Breath is the most crucial part of emotion regulation. The practice creates space between stimulus and response, the ability to pause before reacting (often emotionally). It can be done anytime, anywhere. Extended breathing takes a few seconds or minutes.

Meditation involving deep breathing can, in turn, work as a tranquilizer on the brain and body. This relaxation response can be helpful for sleep quality because the practice lends itself to rest better.

Meditation:
The solution to frustration—an essential key to meditation—is

being in the moment and accepting your thoughts and emotions without judging them. Meditation can be practiced as a deliberate act, an inherent part of many meditative traditions.

How to Meditate

Find a quiet and peaceful place where you can stay on your own. Clear an area where you may collapse, like a cozy chair with a mat, an empty corner, etc. Sit, kneel, or remain lying in the most restful position possible. Whether sitting, place your palms in a relaxed prayer position or put them on your lap, raise your back, and breathe gently. If you are kneeling bow, allow your elbow to lower onto the cushion as you approach the chair. Focus on your posture to create support and equilibrium. Begin with your form, your being. Mentally assess yourself and take notes of the hurtful, anxious, or upset spaces. As you think, you must use one word to refer to the suffering that you see in these fields and let your thoughts remain. Try to persuade your mind that now isn't a time to regret. Give explanations or begin with relief. One might also provide oneself with a cause before meditating. Train your mind to ignore irrelevant thoughts and focus on moving intentionally from your current phase to your goal. Fill your mind with empowering and motivating ideas. Meditate on hopeful and motivational citations, informal guarantees, achievements, joy, joyful ideas, gladness, and light. Imagine discarding all of your dreadful feelings, stress, and bad moods. Breathe these thoughts into your brain. Grin, laugh, make a chuckle, and have a great time suggesting them. Be conscious and purposefully release your stressful contemplations. Picture them to blur away, breathe, and abandon your attitude for tranquility. Focus on the moment; do not allow yourself to stray. You may feel like your temper is sliding away and relaxing.

Since you will be mindful if you have supporting material in your hand or memorized, consider being conscientious of every thought for longer. Notice what guidance these positive thoughts provide as they fill your mind. This way, you gain a little something to bring gentle awareness back to the system of ideas once it starts to wander. When you feel a glimmer of hope, bring ordinary consciousness back. When the grazing is complete, return those thoughts and feelings to their normal state but retain the mindfulness you grew during your practice. When life feels overwhelming, embrace calm through guided meditation once or twice a week. This mindful practice helps release frustration and negativity, allowing you to approach life with a clearer mindset.

Each time you practice releasing anger and frustration with this mindful technique, you develop more excellent emotional stability to navigate life's ups and downs. Thus, a holistic approach to regulating and releasing frustration is formed by combining intentional breathing, body awareness, focus, an attitude of gratitude, and a prayer of thanks.

When we meditate, we learn to regulate our emotions better, so when frustration comes up, it becomes less cumbersome. Being aware of how your emotions are doing can help you notice when frustration starts. Many meditations also include mindfulness, which is present here and now.

Proper time management:
In addition, effective time management helps facilitate the frustrations associated with feeling busy or rushed. Set schedules, establish priorities, and have reasonable expectations to keep your days less frustrating and more manageable. Keeping a journal lets you explore your feelings and understand the reasons behind your frustration. Whether through journaling, poems, or any other form of writing, documenting your thoughts and feelings can be a healthy tool to help you process what you are experiencing and how you react.

Being assertive is the midpoint between passivity and aggression. It involves asserting one's own needs and boundaries while respecting those of others. This can also help avoid frustration when interacting with others. Creating definite boundaries within one's personal and professional life safeguards one's emotional stability and keeps frustration at bay.

MASTERING FRUSTRATION

We encounter frustrating issues daily. Instead of staying stuck, focus on solving the problem. By forcing yourself to solve a problem, you regain agency and diminish some of the emotional damage of frustration. Cognitive restructuring modifies the negative thought patterns of frustration. It reduces the emotional weight of the frustrating parts of your life by fighting against those thoughts and replacing them with more rational ones.

When overwhelmed with frustration, a support group may prove invaluable. Do not shy away from talking to your friends, family, or even your therapist about how you feel. Expressing your grievances can be soothing and help you gain insight into how to deal with unpleasant emotions properly.

Confide in trusted people, friends, and family. They can provide you with understanding, compassion, and a new perspective on whatever adversity you are going through. Saying your frustrations out loud can be therapeutic sometimes, and family members are always available to lend a listening ear or cheer you up.

If your frustration is difficult to overcome, you could seek professional help from a therapist or counselor. A mental health professional can provide guidance, coping strategies and mechanisms, and tools to unpack your emotions better. Therapy provides a safe space to address the root causes of worthlessness and anger.

A support group can help you meet people struggling with similar problems. Support groups can provide a sense of community and understanding online and in person. It can be beneficial and comforting to share with others who have been there, learn coping strategies, and feel less alone.

Connecting with peers who have been through this experience can be excellent. Peer support offers a unique perspective on your frustrations, as people who overcame those same obstacles you are experiencing can provide practical advice based on what worked for them.

Seek online groups or discussion boards where people vent and talk about improper behaviors. These communities provide anonymity and a variety of voices. They also open the door to asking questions, sharing your story, and getting support from a vast network.

Suppose this is happening to you mainly if workplace-related frustrations constitute a significant source of stress. In that case, you may want to take advantage of access through your work, such as with Employee Assistance Programs (EAPs). These programs typically include counseling services and support for employees experiencing life difficulties.

Pursue self-help resources: These can be books, articles, or online materials for controlling frustration. Discovering healthy coping methods and self-care strategies can help you feel more proactive in dealing with your emotions.

Never forget: asking for help is not a sign of weakness; it is the opposite if you feel frustrated. Support from family, friends, or professional help, through informal discussion or finding others in the same situation as yourself, is among the most important things we can have on our journey to control frustration and overcome it.

The strength of these frustration management techniques lies in how often you practice them. You will not be a pro overnight, but with the help of these strategies, you can start managing frustration and work toward being better day by day.

That is, the more you recognize these signs, the better you will be mentally equipped to handle your frustration. You will be better prepared to tackle life with grace and resilience as you practice.

MASTERING FRUSTRATION

Chapter 16

The Power of Effective Communication

Good communication is the transfer of information from one person to another through adequate words, sentences, and thought processes so that the message drifts slowly toward both sender and receiver. It means putting a message as clearly as possible while ensuring a receiver understands what is said and will respond to it positively.

Assertive communication is a style that allows you to express thoughts, feelings, and needs in ways that are clear, direct, and respectful of your context. It also considers the rights and viewpoints of others. It includes self-advocating, boundary-setting, and speaking up.

Assertiveness is a middle ground between passivity and aggressiveness. It means communicating your needs, wants, and limits assertively and respectfully. Being assertive can be a helpful weapon when frustration arises, as it might empower you to express yourself without getting lost in emotional turmoil.

Steps for Assertive Communication:

Becoming an assertive communicator takes time and practice, but your 1:1s will be much better. The following steps will serve as your guide:

Before you tackle the annoying scenario, get clear on your needs and wants. Which result would you be happiest with? An "I" statement is something like this: instead of saying, "You never listen..." say, "When you do not respond when I call out to you... it makes me feel angry." Avoid accusatory statements; instead of saying, "You never come on time," say, "I get angry when I have to wait."

When you are assertively talking, look in the eye of the person you are talking to. This signals confidence and authenticity. Frustration always brings strong emotions, but assertiveness follows a composed and confident disposition. Take some deep breaths to calm yourself down before you say a word.

Listening is also part of assertive communication. Wait until the other person answers if you want to understand. When you are assertive, do not introduce other issues. Address the real problem.

The Sandwich Method:

A great utility in assertiveness is the so-called "sandwich" method. While she is not the originator of the concept, Mary Kay Ash, founder of Mary Kay Cosmetics, brought widespread attention to the sandwich feedback method in the 1980s. This methodology was significant in her 1989 publication, "Mary Kay on People Management." This means surrounding a critical statement with two positive statements. For example:

Tip 1: Start with something nice or complimentary. This puts the card on a friendly note. Key phrases here: in a calm, "I" statement style. End with one more positive comment or compliment. That ends the discussion on a hopeful note.

A sandwich is a feedback delivery method that approaches through the heart and not the head of another. This "sandwich" has three layers,

The Top Bun (Positive Statement): Open with something positive or a compliment. This allows for the feedback to flow much more naturally and without confrontation.

The Filling (Positive Criticism): Write your concerns/feedback in the center. Be specific and clear, using I statements to avoid blaming.

Bottom Bun (Positive Statement): Finish with a positive statement or encouragement. This will give the conversation a positive vibe.

How to Serve a Sandwich — An Example:
Positive Statement (Top Bun): "I want to start by recognizing all the energy and effort you put into this project. It means a lot to the team that you remain committed.

Filler (constructive criticism): "I saw that we are a little behind on the timeline, and I feel it's causing some stress. We have this problem we need to solve to hit our targets.

Bottom Bun (Affirmative Statement) - "I'm sure you care, and moving forward, we can figure it out."

The sandwich technique lets you provide feedback without destroying morale or causing discord. This opens the door to conversation, and the participants will be more open to what you say next.

The Sandwich Technique Advantages:
Starting and closing with concrete positive comments makes the feedback feel less intimidating and minimizes defensiveness. The

sandwich technique differs in that you engage both parties before presenting the solution to the dissemination of frustration, making one part of a structure.

They are problem-solving guidelines more than they are about the problem. The technique preserves relationships and reduces unnecessary conflict by keeping a positive tone.

Attached below are some tips for serving a sandwich successfully:

Before giving your feedback, decide on your positive statements, what your feedback is, and how you will end on a positive note. Provide feedback using "I" statements that explain what you are experiencing/feeling without accusing or blaming. Identify the problem and give examples if you can. Be genuine. Positive statements must be genuine and relevant to the situation. Give constructive feedback and listen to the recipient's response.

Adding the art of serving a sandwich to your assertive communication toolbox is another significant step to frustration mastery. As you slowly learn each new technique and practice it over time, you become closer to feeling free of frustration and living a more emotionally balanced existence.

MASTERING FRUSTRATION

Chapter 17

Your Frustration Detector

When you position yourself like a detective, you can investigate events that trigger frustration and prey on your emotions. This is how you can take on the responsibility to identify the clues, interpret the patterns, and eventually trap frustration before it becomes a part of your life—a road lined with discovery, ah-ha moments, and a better understanding of yourself.

Having finally accepted the journey, you no longer live in the shadow of what influences your life. You have switched on the light, and now you will understand frustration as it happens in layers.

The frustration management is not static; it changes and needs repetition. There are suggestions to keep the momentum going:

Be conscious about logging a status report yourself; notice how you feel. If you recognize frustration, intervening early works best.

MASTERING FRUSTRATION

Like a mirror, this technique offers multiple angles of how you feel and respond. The more you know your frustrated face, the more you will do so with a weapon.

Here is a practical exercise for everyone to kick off this internal reflection.
Think back to a moment in the recent past when you got mad. Assess how intensely you are frustrated. Did it feel like a bit of annoyance, some passing irritability, rage at the fact that life can be so hard to endure?

Think about how you typically react to this particular source of frustration. Do you voice it, bottle it up, or let it bubble under the skin? Think about the impact of your response. Did it enable or disable you from working through the frustration better?

Be open to new skills or tips to help you deal with frustration. Mastery is never really a destination itself. Build a supportive space by surrounding yourself with positive people, reading materials, and resources that motivate you to blossom emotionally.

Self-care is key to emotional resilience. Prioritize sleep, recharge as needed, and enjoy activities that bring you joy. Stay connected with loved ones for essential social support. Focus on nutrition, exercise, and overall health, as physical and emotional well-being are closely linked.

Accepting the Uncontrollable:
Understand that some things in life cannot be controlled or altered. Stop frustrating yourself with things you can not control—some things are out of your reach. An essential step in managing frustration is to accept what you cannot change.

Many instances in life can be irritating but are beyond the content of human touch and power. These situations are most definitely what comes to mind when we imagine things with great feeling and emotion, and yet, no matter how much we want the opposite, fight against it, or feel angry, nothing can change them. Here are some examples of those scenarios:

Earthquakes, hurricanes, floods — and even wildfires are some natural disasters that can wreak havoc and leave devastation in their path. Although we do our best to prevent them, the reality is that these events will happen sooner or later and are out of human control.

Changes in the global economy, recessions, and economic situations affect people and companies. However, those macroeconomic trends don't happen in a vacuum, and they are subject to a wide range of complex forces outside the control of any individual.

Men and women may maintain a healthy lifestyle, but that does not mean they are immune to health problems caused by an inherited genetic condition or disease predisposition. One cannot do much with inherited genetics and upon whom lifestyle choices will be reported.

Aging is a natural process that cannot be avoided, and its physical and cognitive effects can sometimes be annoying. Although healthy habits may play a role in how we age, the rules of aging are human components.

Sometimes, what other people do—particularly those we know best—is annoying until you breathe and question why this happens. However, no one can change another person, and often, they even stop them from doing whatever they do simply because they have autonomy.

Traffic, subway delays, and commuting challenges arrive without warning. No matter how well you try to plan things, your day can still be interrupted when anything else happens that may slow down the trip.

Singular historical events, such as opinion revolutions or geopolitical shifts, affect generations and communities. However, many things influence the course of history, and no one man can make or destroy kings.

Sections across communities and industries face shifting availability of natural resources from drought or commodity prices. Such changes are sometimes an environmental phenomenon that is not immediately visible to humans.

Due to rapid growth in computer technology, massive job losses and a change in the economy and societal structure will occur. Though individuals may cope well with this, the large-scale trajectory of technological progress is determined by many factors.

Life is full of surprises; accidents, sudden illnesses, or unexpected losses can hurt us emotionally and mentally. It is not unusual to slip into such conditions without warning, and they are beyond the human faculties of prediction and control.

Being aware and accepting that such situations are out of our control is a fundamental component of being emotionally resilient. So, instead of trying to change these annoying realities in our lives, finding ways to cope with them and remain positive could mitigate the impact on our emotional well-being due to uncertainty, which is an unavoidable part of life.

Chapter 18

Self-Examination – Your Survey

Why a Frustration Survey?
A survey can usefully illuminate the potentially hidden, slippery phenomenon of frustration. It's like you turn on a light in the middle of the night; suddenly, you see things.

Implementing a survey correctly will really come in handy! It can help identify trends and repetitive patterns in your life that are leading to a lot of frustration.

Frustration usually follows many other feelings. A survey lets you assign numbers and levels to these emotions, providing a more articulated assessment of your feelings.

Answering survey questions honestly helps you identify triggers that frustrate you. This information is crucial for targeted solutions.

You can return to the survey and view your progression as you continue your journey. It is basically a map showing you how far your journey has been based on the dates you have kept track of.

Your Survey of Frustration — For Yourself:
1. What kinds of scenarios or tasks reliably trigger your frustration?
2. What do you usually do to help with how frustrated you feel daily?
3. Do you see any patterns or things that make you frustrated?
4. Where in your life are you under the most pressure, and where does that cause frustration?
5. What are the specific standards, either from you or others, that lead to a trigger of frustration?
6. How do you show your frustration? By behaving, speaking, or bottling up your emotions?
7. Think of a time you were feeling frustrated recently.
8. What triggers your frustration? Is there something in your daily routine or environment that exacerbates the fume?
9. When other people or unexpected events frustrate you, how do you deal with it?
10. When you feel frustrated, does your communication style change? In what ways?
11. Have you been able to utilize frustration as fuel for

something better?
12. But how can you tell the difference between stress that you can work through and frustrating stress?
13. Like tension or restlessness, do you feel any physical expressions of frustration in your body?
14. What are the specific goals or hopes you have that, when unmet, leave you feeling frustrated?
15. In my previous post, I asked how culture has impacted how you deal with frustration.
16. Do you think your reaction to frustration has changed? If so, how?
17. Are there parts of your life where you feel a consistent loss of control, leading to frustration?
18. So, how do you vent and not sacrifice healthy relationships?
19. What are some methods of coping that you have found to work well against frustration?
20. Have you noticed when the mindset you mentally attached yourself to and the frustration level become one?
21. What do you do with setbacks or failures, and what role does that play in your frustration?
22. Do you see your experience of frustration as something that society expects or has set norms for?
23. How does the support—or lack of it—from those around you affect how you cope with frustration?

24. Have you ever experienced change or growth due to deep frustration?
25. Do you have activities that always relieve you of frustration?
26. How will you find the balance between achievement and avoiding frustration?
27. Are there cultural differences in how frustration is taught, understood, and expressed?
28. In what ways has technology, like social media or even the availability of being called at all times by your best friend, exacerbated your frustration?
29. What are some thoughts or beliefs about yourself that make you feel frustrated?
30. If the frustration can not be controlled, did you try different methods to adjust yourself to that observation point or have a better understanding of yourself?

Please consider the examples, such as how you feel and how frustration affects your life, as you answer these questions. It's just part of the process of investigating and identifying frustration.

This survey is only step one. When you're done, you'll better understand where frustration lives. Discover what your frustration is really about and keep moving along the path to mastering it.

Chapter 19

Further Self-Help on Frustration Management

To regulate and cope with our emotions efficiently, we must understand the relationship between frustration and feelings. Emotional regulation involves recognizing, understanding, and controlling one's emotions, allowing individuals to navigate frustration more adaptively. By acknowledging and working through the emotional parts of annoyance, they can learn to resist the reactive patterns it creates, become better at bouncing back from what they see as adverse events, and improve their problem-solving and overall feel-good level.

As time passes, the lessons in emotional life teach people how to cope with unhappiness. Healthy reactions to frustration can help students develop good coping strategies, resilience, and flexibility.

Reflecting on Your Journey:

Consider the journey that you've taken throughout this book more broadly. You have discovered the various masks of frustration, its expense, and how to work with it and shift it. You've navigated the labyrinths of job annoyance, raising children, and contending with adolescents, plus you have learned about stating your case and criticism sandwiching. At this point, you're on your way to conquering the subtleties of this confusing emotion.

More Self-Help Resources:

You may not have to end your journey here. Here are many more resources to help you in your continued journey to frustration mastery:

Many more books on EQ, anger management, and stress relief are available, but those can be used as starting points for better coping with frustration.

1. Unlocking the Unconscious ability to control your emotions
2. A Transformation of the Psyche.
3. Empowered Thinking.
4. Why you Act the Way you Do

5. The Secret (or the Most Important Pillars) to Convert: How to Win a Friend and Become a Powerpuff Girl
6. The Richest Man in Babylon
7. Rich Dad, Poor Dad

Many online classes and workshops are available on emotional management and personal growth, some specifically designed for integrating meditation into daily life. Additionally, different apps and tools assist you in practicing mindfulness, meditation, and emotion regulation.

Conquering frustration takes continual effort. Welcome personal growth and improvement in your journey through life. Overall, you have laid good groundwork, and when faced with difficulties, you'll see them through with grace and poise.

Do not beat yourself up when the result does not come faster than expected. Always remember that personal growth and transformation are an ongoing process. Be patient with yourself, rejoice in the wins, and stay curious about your insights from success and failure. You have the power to control your frustration and live a life that is more balanced, centered, and happy.

An End is a New Beginning:

As you finish this chapter and your journey to mastering frustration, remember that the end of this book is the start of the next chapter in life. You have gained the skills and information you need to prepare for life, embrace growth, and move closer to your journey of emotional mastery.

Now that you've moved from the worst to a slightly better place, let this transformation shape your future of emotional balance, resilience, and growth. This isn't the end—it's just the next chapter in your incredible journey.

Epilogue:

A Letter from the Author

Dear Reader,

As you reach the final pages of this book, I want to express my gratitude for taking this journey towards mastering frustration with me. Throughout these chapters, we've explored the complexities of this often-overlooked emotion, and you've gained valuable insights, techniques, and strategies for managing and transforming it.

Remember that mastering frustration is a lifelong journey, and it's okay to have moments of frustration along the way. What's important is your ability to navigate these moments with grace, resilience, and an understanding of your emotional landscape.

When managed effectively, frustration can be a powerful catalyst for personal growth and positive change. It can lead to increased self-awareness, improved communication, and more harmonious relationships. Frustration can become a teacher that guides you toward greater emotional resilience.

You've acquired diverse tools to assist you on this journey.

Whether deep breathing, assertive communication, providing constructive feedback, or managing the frustrations of children and teenagers, you're well-equipped to handle life's challenges.

Furthermore, I encourage you to embrace ongoing growth and learning. Life is a constant evolution, and your journey towards mastering frustration is part of that journey. Continue to explore new resources, seek support when needed, and always be open to personal growth and transformation.

In closing, remember that the end of this book is the beginning of a new chapter in your life. With your acquired knowledge and skills, you're better prepared to embrace life's challenges and savor its joys.

Thank you for joining me on this adventure of self-discovery and personal growth. I wish you a future filled with emotional balance, resilience, and the fulfillment of your potential.

Sincerely,

Elisha Ogbonna

Other Books

Mastering the Power of Your Emotions: *How to control what happens in you irrespective of what happens in you* - Elisha O. Ogbonna

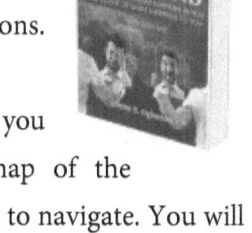

Every day, we are faced with situations that could bring us joy or sadness, love or hatred, fear or confidence. Every event and obstacle in the world around us aims to influence our emotions.

In mastering the power of your emotions, you will be presented with an instructive map of the emotional landscapes many of us are forced to navigate. You will learn the five laws of emotions and discover:

- How temperament and character influence our emotional responses;
- How to respond rather than react to a situation;
- How to handle rejection, abandonment, depression, and grief;
- How to navigate through suicidal thoughts and self-harm behaviors;
- How to handle anonymous threats and various emotional crises;
- How to gain confidence and have a good self-image;
- How to release and replace negative emotions with positive ones

... and a lot more.

A practical, upbeat, and well-organized guide to managing emotions and building resilience and strength... (Kirkus Review March 30, 2018)

The Metamorphosis of the Mind: *Transformative Insights for Winning the Battles of the Mind* – Elisha Ogbonna

Are you looking for a way out of your negative spiral? Discover straightforward techniques for unlocking your hidden natural brainpower.

Do you point the finger at reasons why you failed? Are you fed up with having to make excuses for yourself? Are you struggling to believe in your goal-achieving abilities? Author, teacher, and speaker Elisha O. Ogbonna has taught organizations and individuals for over two decades to tap into our powerful consciousness. He's here to share how you can turn your will into a results-seeking machine and fulfill your greatest dreams.

The Metamorphosis of the Mind: Transformative Insights for Winning the Battles of the Mind is a guide to releasing negativity and redirecting your thinking to support growth. By understanding the three divisions of the intellect and how patterns are formed, Ogbonna sets a detailed map for reinventing your mental success. With intensely practical steps and simple exercises, you'll be inspired to recreate the life of peace and joy you deserve.

In *The Metamorphosis of the Mind*, you'll discover:
- The five powers that differentiate humans from animals and how to turn them to your benefit
- Laws of nature to unleash and accelerate your improved outcomes
- Constructive stimuli to bolster and inspire your progress
- Situations and events that can weaken your mental capacity and how to work around them
- Keys to boosting your inner power, strategies for profound self-discovery, using small things to make significant differences, and much more!

Empowered Thinking: *The Pathway to Self-Discovery and Fulfillment* – Elisha O. Ogbonna

Embark on a transformative journey of self-discovery and empowerment with "Empowered Thinking." In this enlightening guide, Elisha O. Ogbonna delves into the profound exploration of intricate thoughts, thought patterns, and the relationship between the human mind and the transformative force of positive thinking.

Unlike generic self-help books, "Empowered Thinking" offers factual and practical insights for individuals grappling with self-identity, self-discovery, and mental challenges such as indecision, overthinking, confusion, doubt, unbelief, and impacts from discouraging experiences.

As readers progress, they explore "The Act of Thinking," delving into thought patterns, sources of thoughts, and practical tools for cultivating positivity. The guide introduces the five shattering mental barricades, distinguishing between changeable and unchangeable aspects of life and deconstructing cognitive obstacles for a liberated mindset.

Ogbonna presents "Thinking the Right Thoughts" as a strategic blueprint for transcending self-limiting paradigms, urging readers to contemplate broader perspectives on thinking beyond self, fear, size, and societal influence.

This book is not just a guide; it's a transformative roadmap to self-discovery and fulfillment. Elisha Ogbonna equips readers with the knowledge to navigate challenges and embrace positivity for lasting transformation. "Empowered Thinking" is a must-read for anyone seeking to unleash their inner potential and live a life of purpose and meaning.

MASTERING FRUSTRATION

Mastering Success: *How to get to the top and remain there*
– Elisha O. Ogbonna

Are you looking to turn those good intentions into excellent results? Learn how to discover your inner wisdom to create the life of your dreams.

Do you continually hit frustrating hurdles? Does your existence seem stuck at a crossroads? Are you confused about which direction to take to drive better outcomes? Author, teacher, business leader, and speaker Elisha O. Ogbonna has on-the-ground experience in turning stagnant organizations and their people around to achieve their objectives. Now, he's here to share his system for creating breakthroughs so you can reach the pinnacle of your game... without falling back down.

Mastering Success: How to Get to the Top and Remain There is a powerful guide to discovering your perfect fulfillment. In five specific parts that take you through self-discovery and goal-setting strategies, Ogbonna supplies growth and sustainability techniques applicable to every aspect of your life. By following these practical methods, you'll unlock your dream purpose and nail your accomplishments with a winner's ease.

In *Mastering Success*, you'll discover:
- The fundamental principles of self-development to unleash your

hidden powers

- How to set goals to make great results inevitable
- Ways to build community and partnerships to leverage your productivity
- Methods to develop resilience and maintain your focus on peace and happiness
- Tactics for those just starting their journey, ego traps to avoid, business applications, and much more!

Mastering Success is a detailed and practical manual to help anyone forge their future. If you like dynamic thinking, transformational tools, and down-to-earth advice, you'll love Elisha O. Ogbonna's outstanding resource.

Get *Mastering Success* to climb your mountain today!

NOTES

DECISION

MASTERING FRUSTRATION

MASTERING FRUSTRATION

www.ingramcontent.com/pod-product-compliance
Lightning Source LLC
Chambersburg PA
CBHW030905080526
44589CB00010B/151